CAPRICORN 2024

MONTH BY MONTH

Zodiac Odyssey, Published

By Daniel Sanjurjo, 2023.

While every precaution has been taken in the preparation of this book, the publisher assumes no responsibility for errors or omissions, or for damages resulting from the use of the information contained herein.

CANCER ZODIAC SIGN 2024

First edition. November 22, 2023.

Copyright © 2023 Daniel Sanjurjo.

Written by Daniel Sanjurjo.

Introduction

Hello, Capricorn enthusiasts, brace yourselves for a journey into the heart of 2024! This book is your go-to guide for unraveling the celestial mysteries that lie ahead, and we've broken it all down in a language that's as clear as a sunny day.

First things first, we'll dig into the roots of your zodiac sign, uncovering its intriguing history and mythical tales. Ever wondered why Capricorn is associated with the sea-goat or how time got tangled into the cosmic equation? We've got the scoop, and it's as fascinating as it gets!

Next on the agenda – your unique personality traits. From your rock-solid determination to managing that ambitious spirit, we're covering the whole spectrum. Plus, we'll spill the cosmic beans on how you connect with other zodiac signs – the good, the challenging, and the downright interesting.

And that's not all – we'll dive into the hues and gemstones that sync with your Capricorn vibes. Curious about career paths that align with your hardworking nature? We've got the lowdown, whether you're eyeing a leadership role or delving into finance.

But hold tight, we're not stopping there. Ready to navigate the twists and turns of your love life? We've got your back, and for the spicy details, we're delving into Capricorn's romantic prowess – it's about to get intriguing!

Now, the pièce de résistance – your 2024 horoscope. Wondering what the stars have in store for your finances, relationships, and well-being? We've got the details, and we're delivering it in plain and simple English. And for all the Capricorn students out there, get ready to shine because the stars are aligning in your favor!

So, buckle up, Capricorn aficionados! This book is your cosmic roadmap for 2024. It's like having a chat with the universe – straightforward, enjoyable, and brimming with celestial wisdom. Let's make this year one to remember!"

The Capricorn zodiac sign is deeply rooted in the qualities associated with time, responsibility, and a strong sense of tradition. Individuals born under Capricorn, typically between December 22 and January 19, are known for their serious and determined nature, allowing them to navigate the complexities of life with a structured and disciplined approach.

Introduction	2
Capricorn Horoscope 2024	13
Capricorn Career Horoscope 2024	17
Capricorn Love Horoscope 2024	21
Capricorn Marriage Horoscope 2024	24
Capricorn Money & Finance Horoscope 2024	28
Capricorn Health, Family & Children Horoscope 2024	32
January 2024 Capricorn Horoscope	35
February 2024 Capricorn	39
March 2024 Capricorn	42
April 2024 Capricorn	45
May 2024 Capricorn	47
Capricorn in June 2024:	50
Capricorn in July 2024:	53
Capricorn in August 2024:	56
Capricorn in September 2024:	59
Capricorn in October 2024:	62
Capricorn in November 2024	65
Capricorn Personality Traits	72
Capricorn Love, Sex & Compatibility	76
Capricorn Friends And Family	80
Capricorn Career And Money	82
Capricorn Man: A Lover's Guide	88
How to Attract a Capricorn Man:	89

The Capricorn Woman in Love:	92
How to Attract a Capricorn Woman:	93
Capricorn Man: The Ultimate Guide	**96**
Capricorn Man Sexuality	102
Capricorn Man In Relationships	107
Tips for a Successful Relationship with a Capricorn Man:	110
Can You Trust Your Capricorn Man	112
Dating Capricorn Men	116
Understanding Capricorn Men	121
Capricorn Man Likes And Dislikes	127
How To Choose A Gift For Your Capricorn Man	132
Capricorn Woman: The Ultimate Guide	**136**
Love and Relationships:	138
Capricorn Woman In Love	145
Tips for Loving a Capricorn Woman:	149
Capricorn Woman Sexuality	152
Capricorn Woman In Relationships	159
Challenges in Relationships:	162
Can You Trust Your Capricorn Woman	166
Dating Capricorn Woman	172
Understanding Your Capricorn Woman	178
Capricorn Woman Likes And Dislikes	185
How To Chose A Gift For Your Capricorn Woman	**190**
Capricorn History	**195**
The Myth Of Capricorn	199
Capricorn Compatibility	**205**
Capricorn and Aries Compatibility:	205

Capricorn & Taurus	210
Capricorn & Gemini	215
Capricorn & Cancer	220
Capricorn and Leo Compatibility:	225
Capricorn and Virgo Compatibility:	229
Capricorn and Libra Compatibility:	234
Capricorn and Scorpio Compatibility:	239
Capricorn and Sagittarius Compatibility:	244
Capricorn and Capricorn Compatibility:	249
Capricorn and Aquarius Compatibility:	254
Capricorn and Pisces Compatibility:	259

Frequently Asked Questions About Capricorn Men: 270
Capricorn Turn-Ons: 274
Capricorn Turn-Offs: 278
Preferred Gifts for Capricorn: 282
zodiacs adversaries to capricorn 286
Who Gets on Best with of 288
Attractive Traits 291
Negative traits 295
Tailored Self-Care Practices Based on Your Zodiac Sign
299
Ideal Dating Places For Your Partner's Zodiac Sign 303
"Unveiling the Romantic Essence of Every Zodiac Sign"
how romantic they are 307
Why is astrology so provocative? 314
Contact the Astrologer 323
About the Author 330

Key Characteristics of Capricorn:

1. Traditional and Serious: Capricorns are often described as traditional and serious individuals. They value established norms and take a serious approach to their responsibilities and commitments.

2. Inner Independence: Capricorns possess an inner sense of independence that empowers them to make significant progress in various aspects of their lives. This independence allows them to take charge of their personal and professional journeys.

3. Self-Control and Realistic Planning: Capricorns are skilled in self-control and can make realistic plans. Their pragmatic approach enables them to set achievable goals and work steadily towards them.

4. Learning from Mistakes: Capricorns view mistakes as opportunities for learning and growth. They rely on their past experiences and expertise to overcome challenges and achieve success in their endeavors.

5. Material Focus: As an Earth sign, Capricorns are grounded in the material world. They are adept at using resources and focusing on practical matters, contributing to their success in both personal and professional realms.

6. Inflexibility and Stubbornness: The Earth element in Capricorn can make them inflexible and stubborn, particularly in their relationships. They may struggle to accept differences that deviate too far from their own character.

7. Imposing Traditional Values: Capricorns, out of fear, may try to impose their own traditional values on others. This tendency to adhere strictly to their beliefs can create challenges in relationships.

The Symbol - Goat of Fear with a Tail of a Fish:

The symbol associated with Capricorn is the Goat of Fear with a tail of a fish. This symbol represents the decision to protect oneself from perceived threats, whether in the mind, life, or physical surroundings.

Capricorns, like the goat, are always ready to transform themselves to confront and conquer their fears. However, this defensive mechanism can sometimes lead to a cycle of fear and self-protection.

The Ruling Planet - Saturn:

Saturn is the ruling planet of Capricorn, symbolizing all forms of restriction. While Saturn's influence contributes to Capricorns' practicality and responsibility, it can also make them appear cold, distant, and unforgiving. Capricorns may grapple with feelings of guilt or pride, becoming fixated on the past. To foster a more positive outlook, Capricorns need to learn the art of forgiveness and release the burdens of the past.

In essence, Capricorns face the world with bravery, always ready to confront their inner fears and challenges. Their journey involves constant self-transformation and battling their inner monsters, demonstrating resilience and determination in their pursuit of personal and emotional growth.

Capricorn Horoscope 2024

In the coming year, Capricorn is set to embark on a journey of self-discovery and personal growth. The celestial alignments suggest that 2024 will be a transformative period, urging individuals born under the sign of Capricorn to take charge of various aspects of their lives. The overarching theme is one of leadership, with opportunities for inspiring others through individual development and newfound confidence.

Taking the Lead and Inspiring Growth

A prominent feature of the Capricorn horoscope for 2024 is the call to take the lead in all facets of life. This includes both personal and professional domains, encouraging Capricorns to assert themselves and become trailblazers in their chosen fields. The cosmos align to push Capricorns towards leadership roles, where their influence can spark inspiration in those around them. This emphasis on taking the reins signals a period of empowerment and positive change.

Wealth Accumulation and Personal Transformations

Financially, Capricorns can expect opportunities to accumulate wealth through diverse channels in 2024. The celestial configurations favor ventures and endeavors that may yield monetary benefits, providing Capricorns with the chance to enhance their financial stability. Simultaneously, personal lives are marked for significant transformations. The year holds the promise of shedding stressors that may have impeded progress, allowing Capricorns to wrap up pending tasks and move forward unburdened.

Clearing the Path from Grudges and Misunderstandings

Capricorns are also slated to experience resolution in interpersonal relationships in 2024. Lingering tensions from past grudges and misunderstandings will dissipate, creating a conducive environment for building stronger connections. The alignment of celestial bodies suggests that any disruptions caused by historical disputes will find resolution, paving the way for more harmonious and fulfilling relationships.

Embracing Growth and New Horizons

As Saturn influences Capricorn during this period, individuals may find themselves compelled to step out of their comfort zones. This cosmic nudge encourages Capricorns to explore new facets of their personalities. Whether through the pursuit of novel hobbies, redefining approaches to romance, or embarking on adventurous trips with companions, the year invites Capricorns to embrace growth and broaden their horizons.

Cautions on Communication

While navigating these transformative energies, Capricorns are advised to be mindful of their speech. Words carry significant weight, and the impact of communication on relationships cannot be underestimated. It is essential to exercise caution in verbal interactions, ensuring that expressions do not inadvertently harm or strain connections. By approaching communication with sensitivity, Capricorns can navigate the transformative energies of 2024 with grace.

In conclusion, 2024 holds immense potential for Capricorns to thrive, lead, and inspire. By embracing personal growth, navigating financial opportunities, resolving past conflicts, and exploring new horizons, Capricorns can make the most of the transformative energies that define the year ahead.

Capricorn Career Horoscope 2024

The career landscape for Capricorns in 2024 holds promising prospects, characterized by success in business, favorable outcomes from foreign contacts, and the initiation of new projects. The celestial alignments indicate that diligent efforts, especially in resurrecting abandoned projects, will yield positive results, contributing to the overall advancement of Capricorn individuals in their professional journeys.

Promising Signs for Employment

For those already employed, the year brings the potential for a promotion. Recognition for hard work is on the horizon, and Capricorns may find themselves ascending the career ladder with increased responsibilities and opportunities for growth. Moreover, 2024 is deemed auspicious for those considering a change in employment, with the earlier part of the year presenting favorable conditions for job transitions. However, astrological advice suggests exercising caution and avoiding job changes post-October for optimal career stability.

Climbing the Success Ladder

As the year unfolds, Capricorns can anticipate a gradual ascent up the ladder of success in their respective careers. The combination of favorable planetary influences, including the positions of Mars and Jupiter, indicates that success will be a tangible outcome of sustained effort and strategic decisions. The cosmic alignment augurs well for Capricorns, promising achievements and milestones in their professional endeavors by the year's end.

Guidance from Family and Spouse

In matters of career, Capricorns are encouraged to rely on the guidance provided by their spouse and family members. The support and insights offered by close relations will prove invaluable in making informed career choices and navigating challenges. Trusting the wisdom of those around you, especially within the familial sphere, can contribute significantly to the overall success and fulfillment of your professional pursuits.

Politeness in Communication

Effective communication is highlighted in the 2024 Capricorn career horoscope. Capricorns are advised to maintain a polite and diplomatic approach when interacting with others, be it colleagues, loved ones, or superiors. This emphasis on courteous communication serves not only to foster positive relationships but also to create a conducive work environment. By navigating conversations with tact and respect, Capricorns can enhance collaboration and garner support from various quarters.

Overcoming Challenges and Winning Allies

The celestial positions of Mars and Jupiter in the 2024 Capricorn horoscope suggest that challenges will be met with resilience, leading to triumph over adversaries. Capricorns can expect to overcome obstacles in their professional paths, emerging victorious with the support of celestial influences. Additionally, support from government authorities and seniors at work, guided by the influences of Jupiter and Saturn, further fortifies Capricorn individuals against challenges and enhances their prospects for success.

In summary, the career outlook for Capricorns in 2024 is marked by promising opportunities, steady progress, and the potential for significant achievements. By leveraging the support of family, maintaining a courteous communication style, and navigating challenges with resilience, Capricorns can make the most of the favorable cosmic energies propelling them toward success in their professional endeavors.

Capricorn Love Horoscope 2024

The romantic landscape for Capricorns in 2024 is characterized by harmonious connections and shared enjoyment with their partners, influenced by the celestial energies of Jupiter and Venus. This alignment suggests a deep synchronization between you and your partner, fostering a sense of companionship and mutual appreciation. Together, you will revel in each other's company, creating a foundation for a fulfilling and loving relationship.

Creative Ventures and Intimacy

Under the celestial influence of Jupiter and Venus, Capricorns are poised to explore numerous creative ideas to enhance the intimacy with their partners. The year unfolds with a plethora of imaginative plans for travel and shared experiences, contributing to the deepening of emotional bonds. This period offers Capricorns the opportunity to infuse excitement and novelty into their romantic relationships, creating lasting memories with their significant others.

Prospects for Singles

For Capricorns who find themselves single, the year holds the promise of new connections, with a particular emphasis on online interactions. The cosmic alignment suggests the potential for meaningful friendships to evolve into romantic relationships. Singles may find themselves drawn to someone special through digital platforms, and these connections have the potential to blossom into fulfilling love relationships.

Navigating Challenges in Love

Despite the overall positive outlook, the 2024 Capricorn love horoscope does acknowledge potential challenges. There may be instances where decision-making becomes challenging due to confusion, or possessiveness may trigger feelings of stiffness and insecurity in relationships. It is important for Capricorns to be mindful of these potential pitfalls and to approach them with open communication and understanding.

Following the Heart in Love

Throughout 2024, Capricorns are encouraged to follow their hearts when it comes to matters of love and romance. The celestial energies favor authenticity and genuine emotional expression, urging individuals to trust their instincts and emotions. By staying true to themselves and their feelings, Capricorns can navigate the complexities of love with sincerity and openness.

In summary, the love horoscope for Capricorns in 2024 paints a picture of harmonious relationships, creative ventures, and the potential for new love connections. By embracing the opportunities for shared experiences, navigating challenges with communication, and staying true to their hearts, Capricorns can cultivate and enjoy fulfilling romantic relationships throughout the year.

Capricorn Marriage Horoscope 2024

The marital journey for Capricorns in 2024 is influenced by dynamic celestial energies, presenting a mix of increased intimacy and potential challenges. Under the sway of Mars, a surge in physical attraction towards your spouse is foreseen, creating a deeper emotional bond. However, this heightened closeness may coincide with heightened expectations, potentially leading to conflicts, particularly in matters related to intimate acts. The interplay of planetary forces, including the balancing influence of Venus, guides Capricorns through these complexities.

Intimacy and Expectations

The influence of Mars in 2024 brings a notable increase in intimacy and physical attraction within marital relationships for Capricorns. This heightened connection fosters a stronger sense of attachment to your spouse. However, it also brings with it an elevation in expectations, particularly in the realm of intimate acts. This dynamic can potentially lead to conflicts, and here is where the supportive influence of Venus comes into play.

Venus' Balancing Act

The presence of Venus in the cosmic alignment provides a balancing effect on the heightened expectations. Capricorns will find solace and resolution through the harmonizing influence of Venus, helping to overcome any challenges or conflicts arising from divergent expectations. This celestial interplay ensures that the romantic and emotional aspects of the marital relationship are nurtured, contributing to a more harmonious connection.

Navigating Challenges

The middle of the year may pose challenges in the form of misunderstandings that could cause tension in marital life. Mars, with its potent influence, may trigger moments of chaos, testing the stability of the marital bond. It is crucial for Capricorns to be mindful during this period, employing open communication and understanding to address conflicts and maintain the equilibrium in their relationship.

Third-Party Interventions

The 2024 Capricorn marriage horoscope hints at the possibility of third-party interventions causing disruptions in marital relationships. Capricorns are advised to cultivate an atmosphere of trust with their spouses and prioritize spending quality time together. By nurturing trust and communication, couples can strengthen their bond and mitigate the impact of external influences on their marital harmony.

Balancing Temperament

While challenges may arise, other planetary movements are poised to control negative situations and balance temperaments within the marital dynamic. Capricorns are encouraged to approach conflicts with a level-headed demeanor and a commitment to understanding each other's perspectives. By doing so, they can navigate the potential pitfalls and emerge stronger as a couple.

In summary, the 2024 Capricorn marriage horoscope foretells a year of heightened intimacy, increased expectations, and potential challenges. With the supportive influences of Venus and strategic communication, Capricorns can overcome conflicts, navigate external influences, and foster a strong, resilient marital bond throughout the year.

Capricorn Money & Finance Horoscope 2024

The financial landscape for Capricorns in 2024 is marked by a series of opportunities and potential challenges, offering a dynamic interplay of wealth accumulation, controlled expenses, and the promise of financial stability.

Wealth Accumulation and Investments

As per the 2024 Capricorn finance predictions, there are promising opportunities for accumulating wealth through multiple sources. Profits gained during this period are likely to contribute to the multiplication of wealth, especially owing to past investments that yield favorable returns. The celestial support of Jupiter indicates strong prospects for gaining long-lasting ancestral wealth, with a particular focus on profit from land transactions. Capricorns can leverage these opportunities to enhance their financial portfolios.

Controlled Expenses and Family Dynamics

Under the influence of Saturn, expenses are expected to remain generally under control throughout the year. However, the retrograde movement of Saturn from June onwards may introduce challenges, leading to wasteful expenses due to differences within the family. Conflicts, particularly regarding ancestral property, may emerge during this period. Capricorns are advised to navigate these family dynamics with prudence and open communication to maintain financial stability.

Foreign Collaborations and Professional Opportunities

The 2024 Capricorn finance horoscope highlights work related to foreign collaborations, presenting an avenue for assured financial growth. Mars' position further accentuates the potential for professional opportunities in foreign countries. Capricorns may find themselves traveling to international destinations, opening doors to expanded professional horizons and increased financial gains.

Debt Resolution and Financial Stability

The year brings a positive outlook for resolving financial challenges, as indicated by the 2024 Capricorn money predictions. Opportunities to clear financial debts and receive delayed payments will contribute to overcoming past financial problems. Capricorns can expect financial stability throughout the year, providing a solid foundation for exploring diverse avenues for investment with the potential for lucrative returns.

Saturn's Influence and Financial Abundance

Saturn's influence, while it may lead to increased expenditures and potential financial loss, is balanced by the assurance that hard work and efforts will culminate in financial abundance by the year's end. Capricorns are encouraged to approach financial decisions with a strategic mindset, considering the long-term benefits of their actions. The overall trajectory points toward a year of financial growth and stability for individuals born under the sign of Capricorn.

In summary, the 2024 Capricorn money and finance horoscope unveils a year of diverse opportunities, controlled expenses, and the potential for financial stability. By leveraging opportunities for wealth accumulation, navigating family dynamics with prudence, and approaching financial decisions strategically, Capricorns can navigate the financial terrain successfully and conclude the year with a sense of abundance and prosperity.

Capricorn Health, Family & Children Horoscope 2024

The year 2024 brings a dynamic interplay of familial relationships, personal introspection, and health considerations for Capricorns. The celestial influences present a mix of strengthening bonds, potential conflicts, and a need for self-reflection.

Familial Bonds and Aggression

Saturn's position in the 2024 Capricorn family horoscope suggests a strengthening of the bond with your partner or spouse. However, the influence of Mars introduces a note of caution, as it may aggravate aggression, leading to potential opposition from siblings and other family members. Direct and harsh communication may become a challenge, potentially causing disruptions in relationships. Capricorns are advised to exercise patience and temperance in their interactions to maintain familial harmony.

Introspection and Past Mistakes

The year calls for introspection, with the 2024 Capricorn family predictions indicating a need to reflect on past mistakes while enjoying the present. Capricorns may perceive disobedience and a stubborn approach from family members, prompting a thoughtful consideration of whether these responses are reflective of their own behavior. This period offers an opportunity for self-improvement and enhanced understanding within the family dynamic.

Workplace Stress and Family Impact

Stress at the workplace can cast a shadow on family life, according to the 2024 Capricorn family horoscope. Capricorns are encouraged to be mindful of the potential impact of professional pressures on their family relationships. Clear communication and finding a balance between work and family commitments will be crucial to maintaining a harmonious household.

Communication Challenges and Jupiter's Strength

Under the influence of Mercury, Capricorns may face difficulties in communicating with family members and children. It is important to navigate these challenges with patience and open dialogue.

Fortunately, Jupiter's influence offers strength and the ability to accomplish positive things for the family. Capricorns can find solace in providing a sense of protection and stability for their loved ones.

Health Considerations and Psychological Impact

The 2024 Capricorn health horoscope predicts the possibility of chronic health issues and indigestion. The influence of Rahu and Ketu may impact the health of a family member, potentially causing psychological strain. However, by paying attention to diet and fostering positive thoughts, Capricorns can generally maintain good health throughout the year.

In summary, the 2024 Capricorn health, family, and children horoscope present a year of challenges and opportunities for personal growth within the familial sphere. By navigating communication challenges with patience, fostering understanding within the family, and maintaining a focus on health and well-being, Capricorns can navigate the complexities of the year and nurture a supportive and harmonious family environment.

January 2024 Capricorn Horoscope

General Overview: January 2024 heralds significant changes for Capricorns, particularly in the realm of work. Opportunities for involvement in crucial projects or business trips will emerge, propelling career growth. Capricorns' ability to balance emotions and logic becomes an invaluable asset, but continuous control is essential. The Wolf Full Moon encourages a temporary loosening of control, emphasizing the importance of family and conscious choices.

Love: In the midst of career dynamics, Capricorns should prioritize family relationships. The warm atmosphere of the Wolf Full Moon may prompt the cancellation of important meetings, emphasizing the conscious choice of family over professional obligations. This is a time to strengthen familial bonds.

Financial: The first days of January bring success in financial matters, with pleasant surprises and unexpected bonuses. Unforeseen expenses may arise, but

Capricorns will stay financially secure. Loved ones may present valuable gifts, and compassionate influences foster improved relationships, overcoming previous coldness.

Work: Mid-month accelerates career growth with new prospects and opportunities. Capricorns gain clarity on the direction to pursue, identifying valuable connections. The general Capricorn horoscope envisions profitable cooperation and emphasizes the importance of standing out to attract high officials' attention.

Health: Capricorns' mood is influenced by Mercury in Capricorn, fostering clear thoughts and plans. Control over various life aspects ensures a harmonious blend of experiences. Short trips offer refreshing breaks, enhancing overall well-being.

Siblings and Children: Dialogue with loved ones, colleagues, and partners develops positively, presenting an opportune time to strengthen ties. Cooperation is beneficial, and Capricorns should seize every opportunity to stand out. The puzzle of life fragments aligns seamlessly under Capricorn's control.

Summary: January brings transformative energies for Capricorns, particularly in career growth and family connections. Balancing professional and personal life is crucial, with financial successes and unexpected bonuses contributing to overall stability. Capricorns should embrace opportunities for cooperation and stand out to attract favorable attention. The month's end calls for caution in relationships, emphasizing the importance of prioritizing existing bonds over potential flirtations. Overall, luck favors Capricorns, providing a positive mood and successful outcomes. Silver jewelry enhances the beneficial energy radiating through this transformative month.

February 2024 Capricorn

General Overview: February 2024 promises a surge of luck in love for Capricorns, with unexpected meetings disrupting the measured course of life. The Sun in Aquarius introduces a whirlwind of emotions, prompting a beautiful romance that helps break free from complexes. However, caution is advised in financial matters, as reckless actions may lead to potential ruin, especially during the Snow Full Moon when emotions are heightened. Aromatherapy proves beneficial for stress relief.

Love: Capricorns experience a sudden romantic upheaval, bringing forth intense feelings and a brief euphoria. The energy of the Sun in Aquarius disrupts the measured life, and a beautiful romance emerges, providing an opportunity to shed inhibitions and embrace passion.

Financial: The unpredictable nature of early February necessitates preparation for new challenges. Ambitious goals become achievable with effort, and investing in knowledge through training courses is advised. Career-focused Capricorns may need to make sacrifices, but the position of Venus in Capricorn reinforces confidence in imminent triumph.

Work: Career pursuits take precedence in early February, with ambitious goals at the forefront. Strengthening alliances and resuming contacts with colleagues become essential for success. However, enthusiasm may wane by mid-month, requiring attention to shortcomings. Fitness becomes a pleasant solace, and philosophical reflections under Mercury in Aquarius offer a chance to reconcile with past mistakes.

Health: The energy of Mars in Aquarius may bring unbridled energy, contributing to rapid progress but requiring caution to avoid harm. Team fitness training is recommended to channel excess energy positively and maintain overall well-being.

Summary: February brings a mix of romantic excitement and career challenges for Capricorns. The unexpected romance offers a break from routine, but financial caution is necessary. Career pursuits require effort and sacrifice, with alliances playing a crucial role.

Mid-month reflections and fitness activities provide solace, and financial improvements in the month's end bring relief. Team fitness training helps channel excess energy positively.

March 2024 Capricorn

General Overview: March 2024 urges Capricorns to reevaluate family life, addressing pressing issues with a new approach. The Sun in Pisces brings euphoria, making Capricorns ready for challenges and success in business, particularly in creating a profitable startup. Diplomacy and careful preparation open doors, with the Worm Full Moon in March fostering conflict-free negotiations and strengthened business ties.

Love: Early March sparks communication and intriguing acquaintances, inspiring creative achievements. A sudden passion may bring a source of stable income over time. Capricorns, known for their tenacity, fear no barriers. Despite the softness of Venus in Aquarius, opportunities are seized, maintaining order in affairs. Health becomes clearer with preventive examinations.

Family: Mid-March brings pleasant family moments, emphasizing the desire to spend quality time and pamper loved ones. Concessions are advised to avoid disappointment, and addressing domestic disorder leads to a potential new apartment. With Mercury in Aries' support, reorganizing life proceeds smoothly. However, Capricorns should not neglect self-care, as the favorable time for cosmetic procedures arrives.

Career: March signals success in business and creative ventures. Capricorns' firm attitude ensures order, and the support of patrons is secured through diplomatic approaches. The positive end of March signifies the resolution of problems and the emergence of new ideas for a comfortable life. A potential trip requires full preparation, with Mars in Pisces uniting strength and tenderness, promoting an optimistic outlook.

Health: Preventive examinations in early March help detect potential health issues, emphasizing the importance of maintaining well-being. The positive end of the month encourages Capricorns to avoid aggression, engage in meditative practices, and pay attention to self-care.

Summary: March brings a reevaluation of family dynamics and success in business for Capricorns. Euphoria fuels creative ventures, and diplomatic approaches secure support in various endeavors. Mid-March emphasizes family moments and the potential for a new living situation. Successful resolutions and new ideas pave the way for a comfortable life. Health clarity and positive vibrations enhance overall well-being, fostering optimism and attentiveness to self-care.

April 2024 Capricorn

General Overview: April 2024 calls for decisive action, inspiring new achievements and a departure from the shadows. The Sun in Aries encourages dominance, requiring Capricorns to navigate communication tactfully. The Pink Full Moon in April fosters family unity through tenderness and care, resolving differences with a win-win approach.

Love: Financial stability in early April facilitates profitable purchases, and Venus in Aries brings luck in love. Capricorns, typically reserved in emotions, feel a desire to express deeper feelings. A romantic vacation becomes opportune, allowing them to convey the fullness of emotions.

Family: Mid-April brings a wave of spring excitement, prompting Capricorns to try something new and start afresh. Life calls for a journey, and reorganizing life is supported by Mercury in Aries. Amid the hustle, self-care, and cosmetic procedures are recommended to maintain well-being.

Career: The professional sphere yields great achievements in late April, marking the beginning of a rewarding journey. Capricorns should maintain a high pace of work, drawing knowledge from various sources and adopting colleagues' experiences. Mars in Pisces promotes an optimistic outlook, and attentiveness to others fosters positive vibrations.

Health: Amid the spring excitement, Capricorns are reminded to take care of their well-being. Cosmetic procedures become essential for skin recovery, emphasizing the need for self-care. The position of Mars in Pisces encourages avoiding aggression and dedicating time to meditative practices.

Summary: April urges Capricorns to embrace new beginnings with decisive actions. Communication requires tact, and the Pink Full Moon fosters family unity through tenderness. Financial stability allows for profitable purchases, and Venus in Aries brings luck in love. Mid-April prompts a wave of spring excitement, encouraging self-care amid reorganizing life. Late April brings great achievements in the professional sphere, signaling the beginning of a rewarding journey. Capricorns should maintain a high work pace, drawing knowledge from various sources. Mars in Pisces fosters optimism, and positive vibrations result from attentiveness to others and a focus on well-being.

May 2024 Capricorn

Balancing Work and Family in the Month of Taurus

General Overview: May 2024 brings a working mood for Capricorns on the eve of summer holidays. Stability takes center stage, aligning with Capricorn's inner mood. The focus is on pursuing a comfortable life, prompting efforts to earn more. The Flower Full Moon in May peaks activity, but a busy schedule requires attention to health with frequent rest breaks.

Health: The eventful first days of May may impact health, challenging control over life's circumstances. Remaining calm is crucial, as excessive forcing can lead to worsened well-being and potential neurosis. Venus in Taurus encourages Capricorns to drop defenses, presenting an opportunity to improve reputation by showing authenticity. Looking fresh and smart contributes to a positive image.

Work: Mid-May sees a continuous flow of tasks, including household chores. The horoscope advises against getting too caught up in everyday life, emphasizing the fleeting nature of spring. Proper relaxation becomes essential, with the support of Mercury in Aries ensuring smooth proceedings. Capricorns are reminded to balance work with self-care and cosmetic procedures.

Family: At the end of May, despite a busy schedule, family takes precedence. Communication becomes a natural need for some, while others must make an effort to establish contact. The horoscope recommends discussing summer plans, acknowledging potential generational differences and seeking compromise. Under Mars in Aries, a spirit of competition intensifies, requiring strategic approaches for entrepreneurs to navigate disruptions and maintain profits.

Summary: May 2024 urges Capricorns to balance work and family as they navigate a working mood on the brink of summer. Stability and the pursuit of a comfortable life drive efforts, with the Flower Full Moon highlighting peak activity. Health demands attention amid a busy schedule, requiring frequent rest breaks. Venus in Taurus prompts authenticity and image improvement. Balancing work and self-care is emphasized, supported by smooth proceedings with Mercury in Aries. Family takes precedence at the end of May, with communication and compromise essential. Entrepreneurs face intensified competition, requiring strategic approaches for continued success.

Capricorn in June 2024:

The Capricorn horoscope for June 2024 advises against impulsive actions and encourages a well-thought-out action plan. Striving to keep up with everything may lead to unnecessary challenges, so outlining a clear strategy and sticking to it will minimize losses. The energy of the Sun in Gemini brings mental agility, allowing Capricorn to adapt swiftly to changing conditions. A surge of strength empowers them to tackle professional challenges without neglecting personal life, ushering in a period of amorous adventures, especially during the Strawberry Full Moon in June. It's a time for sensual experiments, and Capricorn is encouraged to embrace their desires.

Love: Early June brings a combative mood and heightened self-confidence. Capricorns are urged to cast aside doubts and pursue their goals with determination. Unshakable confidence becomes a catalyst for progress, potentially leading to success in new areas. Venus in Gemini enhances eloquence, making it easier for Capricorn to navigate conflicts and establish friendly relations. It's a favorable time to consolidate successes and build bridges with former adversaries, turning them into allies.

Mid-June: Foresight becomes crucial in mid-June to avoid mistakes. Capricorns are advised to set achievable goals and delegate super-difficult tasks when necessary. Mercury in Gemini contributes to wise decision-making, fostering delight and unbridled optimism. This period allows calculating Capricorns to loosen their control and focus on what resonates with their soul. If there's an opportunity for a trip, it's a good time to seize it, enhancing positive vibrations.

End of June: The calm end of June confirms the wisdom of the chosen strategy. Capricorns can complete projects with measured effort, and the praise from superiors becomes a rewarding affirmation, often translated into monetary terms. Prioritizing the settlement of debts before indulging in expenses is recommended. Capricorns can find reassurance in the patronage of Mars in Taurus for active endeavors. As challenges arise, relying on the mantra "the beginning is half the battle" and envisioning a positive outcome can provide a boost. Tinctures of lemongrass and ginseng are suggested for an energy lift.

Summary: June for Capricorn emphasizes strategic planning, confident action, and embracing sensual experiences. The month holds opportunities for professional success, improved relationships, and financial stability. By maintaining a balanced approach and seizing opportunities wisely, Capricorn can navigate the month with success and fulfillment.

Capricorn in July 2024:

The Capricorn horoscope for July 2024 indicates a peak in communication, offering opportunities for new experiences and lasting connections, particularly during a business trip or a seaside vacation. The focus on family, emphasized by the Sun in Cancer, urges Capricorn to attend to the well-being of loved ones, addressing not only domestic and financial matters but also providing psychological support. The Thunder Full Moon in July propels progress, rewarding even small efforts. Capricorns, accustomed to hard work, will discover the pleasure of self-care, with beauty treatments yielding amazing results.

Love: July brings a surge in communication, presenting opportunities for meaningful connections. The potential for a lifetime union may arise during a business trip or a vacation by the sea. The family takes center stage, and Capricorn's efforts contribute to the overall well-being. The Thunder Full Moon in July adds momentum to progress, making it an ideal time for self-care and beauty treatments.

Financial: The financial situation improves in the early days of July, allowing Capricorns to organize their summer holidays effectively. A chance to secure a budget-friendly tour and additional funds from unexpected sources brings a pleasant surprise. While Capricorns typically appreciate expensive items, the influence of Venus in Cancer softens their temperament, fostering a desire for simple joys. It's a favorable period for everyday tasks, such as updating household appliances and making repairs, enhancing comfort at home.

Mid-July: By the middle of July, preliminary conclusions can be drawn. The Capricorn horoscope suggests that external changes are intertwined with internal transformations. Working on personal growth and cultivating kindness may prove beneficial. Financially, the influence of Mercury in Leo brings good luck, unveiling a new world of wealth and pleasures. Opportunities to participate in lotteries and drawings may surpass expectations, alleviating the need to save.

End of July: The end of July may evoke a sense of déjà vu, prompting contemplation on repeating situations and how to leverage them. Changes in life, possibly a career shift, are on the horizon. While Capricorns are not typically rash, the influence of Mars in Gemini may induce unpredictability. Redirecting energy into creative pursuits is recommended, with active sports providing an outlet for the combination of aggression and frivolity characteristic of this period.

Summary: July for Capricorn marks a period of heightened communication, family focus, and transformative experiences. Opportunities for meaningful connections and financial surprises present themselves. Balancing self-care with family responsibilities and navigating career changes with creativity will empower Capricorns to make the most of this dynamic month.

Capricorn in August 2024:

The Capricorn horoscope for August 2024 ushers in an optimistic mood, promising noticeable shifts in career despite a temporary business lull. Engaging in a promising project brings financial well-being, fueled by growing ambitions under the influence of the Sun in Leo. However, an assertive drive for self-proving may lead to conflicts with relatives, colleagues, and strangers. The Sturgeon Full Moon in August inspires impulsive actions, with unexpected love relationships offering unforgettable sensations.

Love: August brings unexpected love relationships for Capricorn, sparked by impulsive actions inspired by the Sturgeon Full Moon. The romantic atmosphere is enhanced by the optimistic mood, offering a chance for memorable and passionate connections.

Financial: Positive work conditions in early August align with the summer mood, allowing Capricorn to overcome past failures and mistakes. The horoscope advises active engagement and continuous learning to maintain success. The influence of Venus in

Virgo contributes to a harmonious and orderly life, enabling Capricorn to navigate challenges with efficiency.

Mid-August: Despite accumulating fatigue, mid-August propels Capricorn into a responsible business trip with promising prospects. Competition with colleagues is likely, but the potential rewards are bright. Financial luck, courtesy of Mercury in Leo, opens doors to a new world of wealth and pleasures, diminishing the need for frugality.

End of August: A powerful elation at the end of August propels Capricorn towards progress in business, particularly in the real estate sector. Profitable deals, especially in real estate, are on the horizon, promising a significant increase in income. While the influence of Mars in Gemini may induce unpredictability, directing energy towards creative pursuits and active sports is recommended.

Summary: August for Capricorn presents an optimistic period with opportunities for career advancement and financial well-being. The unexpected nature of love relationships adds a touch of excitement. Engaging in a responsible business trip, navigating financial opportunities, and embracing creativity contribute to a successful and fulfilling month.

Capricorn in September 2024:

The September 2024 horoscope propels Capricorn into a dynamic phase, emphasizing hard work for career advancement and financial improvement. The influence of the Sun in Virgo enhances critical thinking, urging a reevaluation of life and the pursuit of personal growth. The Harvest Full Moon in September brings new colors to personal relationships, emphasizing family values and fostering deeper connections.

Love: A transformative period in personal relationships awaits Capricorn during the Harvest Full Moon. Random relationships become a thing of the past, with a focus on family values. Spouses can overcome relationship crises, and single individuals may find happiness in meaningful connections.

Early September: Challenges in early September prompt non-standard actions, testing Capricorn' resilience. Staying on course with planned objectives brings unexpected luck and potential support. Venus in Libra eases the impact of troubles, offering intuitive insights on navigating challenges.

This period encourages self-improvement, including a focus on appearance and a visit to the beautician.

Mid-September: Mood swings in mid-September signal upcoming changes in nature. The horoscope suggests embracing the shift by engaging in travel. Mercury in Virgo accelerates processes and highlights opportune moments. A decisive mindset and final decisions lead to favorable outcomes, especially in resolving housing issues. Great deals and positive developments start unfolding.

End of September: Financial stability characterizes the end of September for Capricorn, with income exceeding expenses. The horoscope predicts stable income, and Capricorn can leverage contacts and a stellar reputation for profitable opportunities. While Mars in Cancer may induce pessimism, Capricorn is encouraged to combat negative feelings. A sachet of lavender can help maintain a positive atmosphere.

Summary: September for Capricorn unfolds as a dynamic and transformative period. Career and financial pursuits require diligence, and personal relationships undergo significant positive changes. Facing challenges with resilience, embracing self-improvement, and seizing opportunities lead to a fulfilling and prosperous month. Financial stability and the potential for lucrative endeavors mark the end of September.

Capricorn in October 2024:

The Capricorn horoscope for October 2024 promises a positive trajectory, with challenges dissipating, supportive allies emerging, and financial prospects soaring. The influence of Libra brings a heightened awareness of others' opinions, propelling Capricorn to take risks for increased prestige. The Hunter's Full Moon in October holds promises of substantial income, prompting considerations for wise fund management, potentially through real estate investments or personal development.

Love: Early October may bring confusion in personal life as high workloads and financial concerns absorb energy, leaving little time for family. The horoscope urges active involvement in family affairs, despite potential challenges. Venus's influence in Scorpio may add emotional complexity, emphasizing the need to stay on course and avoid impulsive decisions. Cleaning and decluttering serve as effective ways to maintain mental clarity.

Mid-October: The pace quickens by mid-October, presenting Capricorn with new projects, intriguing individuals, and an influx of information. Monitoring superiors' reactions becomes crucial, as their approval shapes future events. Mercury in Scorpio introduces spontaneity, temporarily alleviating Capricorn's usual restraint. The month encourages embracing new hobbies, possibly delving into extreme sports to expand personal boundaries.

End of October: Positive developments mark the end of October, attributed to intentional actions rather than random chance. The horoscope emphasizes spiritual comfort for Capricorn, prioritizing pure thoughts and a kind heart. While Mars in Cancer may bring unexpected challenges, Capricorn's strong will and character can overcome them. Balancing internal resources is crucial, with meditation on a candle flame suggested for replenishing strength.

Summary: October unfolds positively for Capricorn, with financial prospects on the rise and challenges dissipating. The focus on prestige and increased income aligns with the Hunter's Full Moon, prompting considerations for wise fund management. In personal life, active involvement in family affairs is encouraged, despite potential hurdles. The accelerated pace in mid-October brings new opportunities and challenges, emphasizing the importance of monitoring superiors' reactions. The month concludes with positive developments, underscoring the significance of spiritual comfort and maintaining internal balance. Meditation serves as a valuable practice for rejuvenating internal resources.

Capricorn in November 2024

The Capricorn horoscope for November 2024 predicts a bustling period filled with both professional engagements and opportunities for personal enjoyment. Despite the busy schedule, there's ample time for pleasurable activities to lift spirits during the autumn season. The influence of the Sun in Scorpio enhances sensuality, granting free-spirited Capricorns the green light for love. Socializing and taking the initiative in communication are encouraged, although caution is advised to navigate potential intrigues during the Beaver Full Moon in November.

Love: The Beaver Full Moon may introduce a practical approach to thoughts in relationships, with pragmatic Capricorns hesitant to sacrifice their career for personal life. While a cooling period might occur, it's expected to be temporary. The horoscope suggests being more visible in public, taking the lead in communication, and overcoming misunderstandings with compassion.

Early November: Early November is marked by a flurry of events and news, prompting Capricorns to focus on the most important aspects of life, such as learning a foreign language. The influence of Venus in Sagittarius fosters compassion, facilitating the resolution of misunderstandings in relationships. This period is opportune for strengthening ties with loved ones, colleagues, and partners.

Mid-November: The situation improves by mid-November, allowing for the resolution of most tasks and impressive achievements. The stable financial situation sets the stage for self-reflection and preparation for upcoming holidays. Under the influence of Mercury in Sagittarius, clarity emerges, and Capricorns find solutions to previously perceived insoluble problems related to inheritance, deposits, or real estate.

End of November: The bustling end of November signals the approach of the holidays, encouraging Capricorns to focus on the temporary nature of the situation. The horoscope recommends starting an advent calendar for both practical and decorative purposes. Mars in Leo serves as an additional advantage in job hunting or relocation, transforming closed Capricorns into excellent conversationalists. The adaptation process is anticipated to be smoother than expected.

Summary: November unfolds as a bustling yet dynamic month for Capricorn, offering a balance between professional engagements and personal enjoyment. Love and relationships may face practical considerations, but the horoscope encourages visibility, communication, and compassion to navigate potential challenges. Early November prompts a focus on essential aspects of life, with opportunities for language learning and relationship strengthening. Mid-November brings improvements and financial stability, fostering self-reflection and holiday preparation. The lively end of November sets the stage for the holidays, with practical and decorative advent calendars recommended. Mars in Leo enhances communication skills and facilitates a smoother adaptation process.

December 2024 Capricorn Horoscope Guide: A Cosmic Finale

General Overview: The concluding month of 2023 brings success to Capricorns, especially in financial endeavors. However, an inflated sense of self-importance could lead to complications, particularly in personal relationships. Exercise caution in new connections to avoid deception. Health-wise, focus on nutrition to combat potential exacerbation of chronic conditions during the Cold Full Moon.

Love: Venus in Libra emphasizes aesthetics, fostering a desire to enhance beauty in life. Capricorns may find joy in cultural pursuits like museum visits. Relationship stability is supported, but be mindful of the influence of appearances on decisions.

Family: Maintain harmony in family life, but be cautious of potential deceit from acquaintances. Clear toxic elements from your surroundings. Consider addressing the desire for a change in residence. Mercury in Capricorn ensures clear thoughts and plans, allowing you to navigate potential challenges.

Marriage: Capricorns may face dishonest behavior from acquaintances, prompting a reevaluation of plans. The influence of Mercury aids in clear thinking. If the urge to change residence arises, explore the possibility. Short trips can refresh the spirit and combat any lingering melancholy.

Financial: Fluctuations in finances are expected. The Capricorn horoscope advises building a financial cushion for stability. Embrace the influence of Venus in Libra, prioritizing aesthetics. Small savings can offer confidence and protect against unforeseen challenges.

Work: Mid-month brings potential plan adjustments based on new information. Some acquaintances may engage in intrigues, requiring clearing of toxic elements. Capricorn's control and clear thinking, driven by Mercury, enable them to adapt and maintain control. Consider a short trip to alleviate any emotional burden.

Health: The Cold Full Moon may impact chronic conditions; prioritize a balanced diet with more vegetables, fruits, and whole grains. Capricorns should be mindful of their well-being and take preventive measures.

Siblings and Children: Maintain clear communication with siblings, as Mercury's influence aids in understanding. Children may benefit from a well-thought-out celebration, creating warm memories. Capricorns can harness Mars in Sagittarius to embark on unique endeavors, balancing impulsivity through physical activities.

Summary: December brings financial success, aesthetic pursuits, and relationship stability for Capricorns. Adaptability and clear thinking are key to navigating potential challenges. Embrace the festive spirit and cherish warm celebrations with loved ones. A cosmic finale awaits, with the potential for new beginnings in the coming year.

Capricorn Personality Traits

Capricorn is the tenth sign of the zodiac, represented by the symbol of the Goat. Individuals born between December 22 and January 19 fall under this sign. Capricorn is an Earth sign, along with Taurus and Virgo, and is ruled by the planet Saturn. Here are some key personality traits associated with Capricorns:

1. Ambitious: Capricorns are known for their strong ambition and desire for success. They are willing to work hard and persistently toward their goals, often aiming for long-term achievements.

2. Disciplined: Capricorns exhibit a disciplined and responsible nature. They are capable of managing their time effectively and are often seen as reliable individuals who can be trusted with responsibilities.

3. Practical: Grounded in practicality, Capricorns are realistic and pragmatic in their approach to life. They prefer to deal with concrete facts and are adept at finding practical solutions to problems.

4. Patient: Capricorns are patient individuals who understand the value of time and effort. They are willing to wait for the fruits of their labor and can endure challenges with a steadfast demeanor.

5. Organized: Order and organization are important to Capricorns. They thrive in structured environments and appreciate planning and methodical approaches to tasks.

6. Cautious: Capricorns tend to be cautious in their decision-making. They carefully weigh the pros and cons before taking action, avoiding impulsive choices that may lead to unnecessary risks.

7. Reserved: Capricorns can be reserved and may not readily express their emotions. They value privacy and often keep their feelings guarded until they feel comfortable opening up.

8. Traditional: Capricorns often have a respect for tradition and may appreciate conventional values. They may find stability and security in adhering to established norms and practices.

9. Resourceful: Capricorns are resourceful individuals who can make the most of what they have. They are adept at finding practical solutions and navigating challenges with a strategic mindset.

10.   Independent: While Capricorns value relationships, they also cherish their independence. They are self-sufficient and prefer to rely on their own abilities to achieve their goals.

11.   Determined: Once Capricorns set their sights on a goal, they are determined to achieve it. They possess a strong sense of purpose and resilience in the face of obstacles.

12.   Witty Sense of Humor: Despite their often serious demeanor, Capricorns can have a dry and witty sense of humor. They appreciate cleverness and intelligence in comedy.

It's important to note that while these traits are commonly associated with Capricorns, individual personalities can vary based on factors such as upbringing, life experiences, and the influence of other astrological elements in a person's birth chart.

Capricorn Love, Sex & Compatibility

Love and Relationships for Capricorns: Capricorns approach love with the same seriousness and commitment they bring to other aspects of their lives. They value stability and are likely to seek a partner who shares their dedication to long-term goals. While they may not easily express their emotions, once committed, Capricorns are loyal and reliable partners. They appreciate partners who are equally responsible and can contribute to a secure and structured home life.

Sexuality for Capricorns: In the realm of sexuality, Capricorns can be reserved initially, but their sensuality deepens as trust and emotional connection grow. They often view sex as a way to strengthen the bond in a relationship rather than a mere physical act. Capricorns tend to be patient and attentive lovers, valuing quality over quantity. They may not be overly experimental but strive to create a secure and intimate atmosphere for their partner.

Compatibility with Other Signs:

- **Best Matches:**

- Taurus: Both Earth signs, Taurus and Capricorn share a practical approach to life. They appreciate stability and are likely to build a strong, long-lasting relationship.

- Virgo: Another Earth sign, Virgo aligns well with Capricorn's values of responsibility and organization. Their shared commitment to practicality can create a harmonious partnership.

- **Good Matches:**

- Pisces: Capricorn's grounded nature complements Pisces' dreaminess. While differences exist, their unique strengths can balance each other.

- Scorpio: The intense Scorpio can intrigue Capricorn. Both signs value commitment, and their compatibility can stem from shared long-term goals.

- **Challenging Matches:**

- Capricorn: Aries' impulsive nature may clash with Capricorn's careful planning. They have different approaches to life that may require compromise and understanding.

- **Gemini:** Capricorn's serious demeanor contrasts with Gemini's light-heartedness, potentially leading to misunderstandings.

Love Tips for Capricorns:

1. **Express Emotions:** While it may not be their natural inclination, Capricorns can benefit from expressing their emotions more openly to deepen their connections.

2. **Balance Work and Love:** Capricorns' dedication to their careers can sometimes overshadow their relationships. Finding a balance between work and personal life is crucial.

3. **Appreciate Differences:** Instead of trying to impose their own values, Capricorns can benefit from appreciating and understanding the differences in their partners.

In summary, Capricorns approach love and relationships with a serious and committed mindset. Their compatibility with other signs often hinges on shared values and goals. While challenges may arise, Capricorns can foster fulfilling relationships by expressing their emotions, finding balance, and appreciating the uniqueness of their partners.

Capricorn Friends And Family

Friends: Capricorns are known for being reliable and loyal friends. They may not have a large circle of friends, but the ones they do have are usually long-lasting. Capricorns value quality over quantity in friendships. They are the type of friends who will be there in times of need, offering practical advice and support. While they may not be the most expressive or emotionally demonstrative, their actions speak volumes about their commitment to their friends. Capricorns appreciate friends who share their values of responsibility and ambition.

Family: Family is of utmost importance to Capricorns. They are likely to take on responsibilities within the family structure, and they strive to create a stable and secure home environment. Capricorns often have a strong sense of tradition and may value family customs and rituals. While they may seem reserved in expressing their emotions, their dedication to family is unwavering. They are often the ones organizing family events, ensuring everyone's well-being, and acting as a reliable anchor for their family members.

Parenting: As parents, Capricorns are likely to instill a sense of discipline, responsibility, and work ethic in their children. They are concerned with providing a secure and structured environment for their family. While they may have high expectations, they also offer guidance and support to help their children succeed in life. Capricorns may find it challenging to openly express affection, but their actions demonstrate their deep love and commitment to their family.

Challenges: Capricorns may face challenges in expressing their emotions openly, which can sometimes create misunderstandings in relationships. They may need to consciously work on communicating their feelings to ensure that their friends and family understand their emotional depth. Additionally, their focus on work and responsibility may sometimes lead to them being perceived as too serious or distant.

Tips for Stronger Relationships:

1. **Communication:** Capricorns can benefit from opening up more emotionally

and communicating their feelings to strengthen their relationships.

2. Balance Work and Personal Life: Finding a balance between work and personal life is crucial for Capricorns to ensure they can devote time to both their career and relationships.

3. Appreciate Moments: Capricorns should learn to appreciate and enjoy the present moments with friends and family, not just focusing on future goals.

In conclusion, Capricorns are steadfast and dedicated friends and family members. Their loyalty, reliability, and commitment contribute to creating a strong support system for those fortunate enough to be part of their inner circle.

Capricorn Career And Money

Career for Capricorns:

1. Ambitious Leaders: Capricorns are ambitious and driven individuals who aspire to climb the professional ladder. They often set high goals for themselves and work diligently to achieve them.

2. Disciplined Workers: Known for their discipline, Capricorns approach their work with a structured and organized mindset. They are reliable and can be counted on to meet deadlines and fulfill responsibilities.

3. Strategic Planners: Capricorns are excellent planners. They carefully strategize their career moves and are not afraid to put in the hard work required to reach their objectives.

4. Responsible Team Members: In team settings, Capricorns are responsible and contribute to the overall success of the group. They take their duties seriously and can be trusted to deliver results.

5. Thriving in Traditional Professions: Capricorns may excel in traditional professions such as finance, law, management, or any field that requires strategic thinking, planning, and responsibility.

Money for Capricorns:

1. **Financial Stability:** Capricorns value financial stability and security. They are diligent savers and planners, making them well-prepared for unexpected expenses or future investments.

2. **Long-Term Investments:** Capricorns are likely to invest in long-term ventures. They carefully consider their financial decisions, aiming for lasting returns rather than quick gains.

3. **Cautious Spenders:** While they appreciate the finer things in life, Capricorns are generally cautious spenders. They prefer to spend on items of value and quality rather than indulging in impulsive purchases.

4. **Earning Respect:** Capricorns often associate their self-worth with their professional achievements and financial success. Earning respect in the workplace is crucial to their overall sense of accomplishment.

5. **Balancing Work and Personal Finances:** Capricorns understand the importance of balancing work and personal finances. They are likely to create budgets, set

financial goals, and stick to a disciplined approach to money management.

Challenges:

1. Workaholic Tendencies: The dedication Capricorns have towards their careers can sometimes lead to workaholic tendencies. It's important for them to find a balance between professional success and personal well-being.

2. Fear of Failure: Capricorns' fear of failure may lead them to overwork or be overly cautious. Learning to embrace setbacks as opportunities for growth is crucial for their overall development.

Tips for Career and Money Success:

1. Balance Work and Life: Capricorns should strive to maintain a healthy work-life balance to avoid burnout and ensure overall well-being.

2. Embrace Change: While Capricorns are skilled planners, they should also be open to change and adaptability in their careers to seize new opportunities.

3. Invest Wisely: Capricorns should continue their careful approach to investments but be open to exploring diverse opportunities for financial growth.

4. Celebrate Achievements: Taking the time to celebrate career milestones and financial successes is essential for Capricorns to recognize their hard work and accomplishments.

In summary, Capricorns are ambitious and disciplined individuals who approach their careers with a strategic mindset. They value financial stability, are responsible with money, and tend to excel in traditional professions. Balancing work commitments with personal well-being and embracing change are essential for their continued success in both career and finances.

Capricorn Man: A Lover's Guide

The Capricorn Man in Love:

1. Serious and Committed: The Capricorn man approaches love with the same seriousness he applies to other aspects of his life. Once he commits, he is in it for the long haul.

2. Steadfast and Reliable: Known for his reliability, the Capricorn man is a steady and dependable partner. He values stability in relationships and strives to create a secure environment.

3. Patient and Persistent: Capricorn men are patient and persistent in pursuing the object of their affection. They understand that genuine connections take time to develop.

4. Ambitious Partner: Ambition is a hallmark of the Capricorn man's personality. He appreciates a partner who shares his drive for success and is supportive of his career aspirations.

5. Reserved Expression of Emotions: Capricorn men may not express their emotions openly, but their actions speak volumes. They show love through practical gestures and acts of service.

How to Attract a Capricorn Man:

1. Demonstrate Ambition: Capricorn men are attracted to individuals who are ambitious and have a clear sense of direction in life. Showcasing your own goals and drive will catch his attention.

2. Be Patient: Building a connection with a Capricorn man takes time. Be patient, as rushing the process may not be well-received.

3. Show Reliability: Reliability is crucial for a Capricorn man. Demonstrate your dependability through consistent actions and keeping your commitments.

4. Respect Tradition: Capricorn men often appreciate tradition and stability. Showing respect for traditional values can create a strong foundation for a relationship.

5. Share Intellectual Conversations: Capricorns value intelligence and thoughtful conversations. Engaging in discussions about meaningful topics will appeal to his intellectual side.

Challenges in a Relationship with a Capricorn Man:

1. **Reserved Nature:** The Capricorn man's reserved nature may make it challenging for him to express emotions openly. Patience and understanding are key to navigating this aspect.

2. **Workaholic Tendencies:** Due to their ambitious nature, Capricorn men may become absorbed in their work. Balancing career and relationship requires effective communication.

3. **Fear of Failure:** Capricorn men may have a fear of failure, impacting their willingness to take risks in love. Encouraging them to embrace vulnerability is essential.

Keeping the Relationship Strong:

1. **Celebrate Achievements:** Acknowledge and celebrate each other's achievements, as success is crucial for a Capricorn man's sense of self-worth.

2. **Communicate Openly:** Encourage open communication about feelings and emotions. Creating a safe space for vulnerability strengthens the bond.

3. **Find Balance:** Help the Capricorn man find a balance between work and personal life. Supporting his ambitions while ensuring time for relaxation is important.

4. **Build Trust:** Trust is fundamental for a Capricorn man. Be honest, reliable, and consistent to build a foundation of trust in the relationship.

In conclusion, the Capricorn man is a serious and committed partner who values stability and reliability in a relationship. Demonstrating ambition, patience, and understanding can help attract and maintain a strong connection with this steadfast and determined individual.

Capricorn Woman: A Lover's Guide

The Capricorn Woman in Love:

1. **Determined and Committed:** The Capricorn woman is known for her

determination and commitment in love. Once she decides on a partner, she is likely to be dedicated and loyal.

2. Practical and Grounded: Capricorn women approach love with a practical mindset. They value stability and are attracted to partners who share their grounded approach to life.

3. Patient in Relationships: Capricorn women are patient when it comes to relationships. They understand the importance of time in building a strong and lasting connection.

4. Ambitious Partner: Similar to Capricorn men, Capricorn women appreciate a partner who is ambitious and shares their drive for success. They are likely to be supportive of their partner's career goals.

5. Expressing Love through Actions: Capricorn women may not be overly expressive with words, but they show their love through practical gestures and acts of service.

How to Attract a Capricorn Woman:

1. **Demonstrate Ambition:** Capricorn women are attracted to ambitious individuals who have clear goals and aspirations. Showcasing your own drive for success can capture her attention.

2. **Show Stability:** Stability is key for a Capricorn woman. Demonstrating reliability and a grounded approach to life will appeal to her practical nature.

3. **Be Patient:** Building a connection with a Capricorn woman takes time. Be patient and allow the relationship to develop naturally.

4. **Respect Her Independence:** Capricorn women value their independence. Show respect for her need to pursue personal and professional goals alongside the relationship.

5. **Engage in Meaningful Conversations:** Capricorn women appreciate intellectual conversations. Engage in discussions about important topics to stimulate her mind and demonstrate compatibility.

Challenges in a Relationship with a Capricorn Woman:

1. **Reserved Nature:** Capricorn women may have a reserved nature, making it challenging for them to express emotions openly. Creating a safe space for vulnerability is essential.

2. **Workaholic Tendencies:** Due to their ambitious nature, Capricorn women may become absorbed in their careers. Balancing work and relationship requires effective communication.

3. **Fear of Failure:** Capricorn women may harbor a fear of failure, impacting their willingness to take risks in love. Encouraging them to embrace vulnerability and take emotional risks is important.

Keeping the Relationship Strong:

1. **Celebrate Achievements:** Acknowledge and celebrate each other's achievements, as success is crucial for a Capricorn woman's sense of self-worth.

2. **Encourage Open Communication:** Foster an environment of open

communication. Encourage her to express her feelings and thoughts openly, and reciprocate in kind.

3. Support Career Goals: Understand and support her career goals and ambitions. A supportive partner who encourages her professional growth is likely to strengthen the relationship.

4. Find Balance: Help the Capricorn woman find a balance between work and personal life. Encourage relaxation and quality time together to maintain a healthy relationship.

In summary, the Capricorn woman is a determined and committed partner who values stability and ambition in a relationship. Demonstrating ambition, stability, patience, and open communication can contribute to a strong and enduring connection with this practical and loyal individual.

Capricorn Man: The Ultimate Guide

Capricorn Man: The Ultimate Guide

The Capricorn man is characterized by his ambitious and disciplined nature. Born between December 22 and January 19, he belongs to the Earth element and is ruled by the planet Saturn. Here's a comprehensive guide to understanding the Capricorn man in various aspects of life:

Personality Traits:

1. **Ambitious:** Capricorn men are driven by a strong desire for success and achievement. They set high goals for themselves and are willing to work hard to attain them.

2. **Disciplined:** Known for their disciplined approach, Capricorn men are organized and methodical in their actions. They thrive in structured environments and appreciate order.

3. **Patient:** Patience is a virtue for Capricorn men. They understand the importance of time and are willing to wait for the results of their hard work.

4. **Responsible:** Responsibility is a key trait. Capricorn men take their duties

seriously, whether in their professional or personal lives, and are reliable individuals.

5. Reserved: Capricorn men can be reserved in expressing their emotions. While they may not show their feelings openly, they demonstrate their love and commitment through actions.

Love and Relationships:

1. Serious Commitment: Capricorn men approach love with a serious and committed mindset. They are not ones for frivolous relationships and seek a partner for the long term.

2. Loyal and Reliable: In a relationship, the Capricorn man is loyal and reliable. He values stability and creates a secure environment for his partner.

3. Expressing Love: While not overly expressive verbally, Capricorn men express love through practical gestures and acts of service. They are dependable and supportive partners.

4. Patient Pursuit: Capricorn men are patient when pursuing a romantic interest.

They believe in allowing relationships to develop naturally over time.

5. Balancing Work and Love: Work is essential for a Capricorn man, but he understands the importance of balancing professional success with a fulfilling personal life.

Career and Ambition:

1. Ambitious Professional: Capricorn men are highly ambitious in their careers. They set clear goals, plan strategically, and work diligently to achieve success.

2. Disciplined Worker: Known for their disciplined work ethic, Capricorn men are reliable team members who can be counted on to meet deadlines and fulfill responsibilities.

3. Strategic Planner: The ability to plan strategically is a strength. Capricorn men carefully consider their career moves and aim for long-term success.

4. Career Success: Capricorn men often find success in traditional professions such as finance, law, management, or any field that requires planning and responsibility.

5. Balancing Work and Personal Life: While dedicated to their careers, Capricorn men recognize the importance of balancing work commitments with personal life to maintain overall well-being.

Friendship:

1. Quality Over Quantity: Capricorn men value quality over quantity in friendships. They may have a small circle of friends, but these connections are deep and enduring.

2. Reliable Friend: Known for their reliability, Capricorn men are the friends you can count on in times of need. They offer practical advice and unwavering support.

3. Loyalty: Loyalty is a significant trait in friendships. Capricorn men are dedicated to their friends and value the trust that comes with these relationships.

4. Patient Listener: In friendships, Capricorn men are patient listeners. They provide a steady and supportive presence, often offering practical solutions to problems.

5. Respect for Tradition: Capricorn men may appreciate traditional values in friendships, valuing the stability and enduring qualities of long-term connections.

Challenges and Growth:

1. Reserved Nature: Capricorn men's reserved nature may sometimes hinder open communication. Learning to express emotions more openly can contribute to personal growth.

2. Workaholic Tendencies: The dedication to their careers may lead to workaholic tendencies. Striking a balance between professional success and personal well-being is essential.

3. Fear of Failure: Capricorn men may struggle with a fear of failure, impacting their willingness to take risks. Embracing setbacks as opportunities for growth is crucial.

4. Opening Up Emotionally: Learning to open up emotionally and share feelings with loved ones can help overcome challenges related to their reserved nature.

Conclusion:

The Capricorn man is a complex and multi-faceted individual, driven by ambition, discipline, and a sense of responsibility. Understanding his traits, both strengths and challenges, is essential for building strong connections in love, friendships, and professional relationships. As with any zodiac sign, individual personalities may vary, but this guide provides a broad overview of the typical characteristics of a Capricorn man.

Capricorn Man Sexuality

Capricorn Man Sexuality: Unveiling His Passionate Nature

The sexuality of a Capricorn man is a fascinating blend of sensuality, dedication, and a deep connection between the physical and emotional aspects of intimacy. Here's a closer look at the sexual traits and preferences that often characterize a Capricorn man:

1. Sensual and Patient Lover:

- A Capricorn man approaches sex with a sensual and patient demeanor. He values quality over quantity and is likely to invest time and effort to create a meaningful connection.

2. Deep Emotional Connection:

- For a Capricorn man, sex is not merely a physical act but an expression of a profound emotional connection. He seeks a partner with whom he can share both the physical and emotional aspects of intimacy.

3. Reserved at First:

- Capricorn men can be reserved initially, especially when it comes to expressing their desires openly. Building trust and comfort is essential for them to fully open up in the bedroom.

4. Traditional Values:

- Rooted in traditional values, a Capricorn man often appreciates a committed and stable relationship. He tends to express his sexuality within the bounds of a meaningful and long-term connection.

5. Physical Stamina:

- Capricorn men are known for their physical stamina and endurance. They approach sexual encounters with a dedicated and enduring spirit, aiming to satisfy both themselves and their partner.

6. Appreciation for Quality:

- Quality matters to a Capricorn man in all aspects of life, including sex. He appreciates a partner who values the importance of a satisfying and intimate connection.

7. Comfort and Security:

- Capricorn men thrive in an environment of comfort and security. Feeling emotionally safe and supported enhances their sexual experiences and allows them to fully express their desires.

8. Need for Emotional Connection:

- Emotional intimacy is a crucial component of a Capricorn man's sexual satisfaction. He seeks a partner who can connect with him on a deep emotional level, fostering trust and vulnerability.

9. Conservative Approach:

- In some cases, Capricorn men may exhibit a more conservative approach to sexual exploration. They prefer to stick to what they know and enjoy, gradually introducing new elements as trust and comfort develop.

10. Aiming for Mutual Satisfaction:

- The satisfaction of both partners is a priority for a Capricorn man. He appreciates communication and feedback, striving to ensure that the sexual experience is enjoyable and fulfilling for both himself and his partner.

Tips for a Fulfilling Sexual Relationship with a Capricorn Man:

1. Build Emotional Connection: Foster a deep emotional connection to enhance the intimacy between you and the Capricorn man.

2. Express Your Desires: Encourage open communication about desires and fantasies to create a space for exploration and understanding.

3. Create a Comfortable Environment: Ensure a comfortable and secure environment that allows the Capricorn man to feel at ease and fully express himself.

4. Celebrate Intimacy: Appreciate and celebrate the intimate moments, emphasizing the emotional and physical connection shared between you and your Capricorn partner.

5. Be Patient: Capricorn men value patience in the development of a sexual relationship. Take the time to build trust and gradually explore new aspects of intimacy.

Remember, individual preferences vary, and while these traits may be commonly associated with Capricorn men, it's crucial to communicate openly with your partner to understand and fulfill each other's needs and desires.

Capricorn Man In Relationships

Capricorn Man in Relationships: A Guide to Understanding His Approach

When it comes to relationships, the Capricorn man brings a unique blend of dedication, stability, and ambition. Understanding his traits and tendencies can pave the way for a strong and enduring connection. Here's a comprehensive guide to the Capricorn man in relationships:

1. Dedicated and Committed:

- The Capricorn man is known for his unwavering dedication and commitment in relationships. When he decides to be with someone, he approaches it with a serious and long-term mindset.

2. Stable and Reliable Partner:

- Stability is a cornerstone of the Capricorn man's approach to relationships. He values reliability and strives to create a secure and predictable environment for his partner.

3. Building a Strong Foundation:

- Capricorn men are methodical in their approach to relationships, focusing on building a strong foundation. They take time to understand their partner, allowing the connection to develop organically.

4. Expressing Love Through Actions:

- While not overly expressive verbally, a Capricorn man expresses love through practical gestures and acts of service. He believes in demonstrating his commitment through reliable actions.

5. Balancing Work and Personal Life:

- Work is essential for the Capricorn man, but he understands the importance of balancing professional success with a fulfilling personal life. Finding this balance is crucial for a harmonious relationship.

6. Supportive and Encouraging:

- In a relationship, a Capricorn man is supportive of his partner's goals and ambitions. He appreciates a partner who shares a similar drive for success and encourages personal growth.

7. Patient and Understanding:

- Patience is a virtue for the Capricorn man. He understands that relationships require time to deepen, and he approaches challenges with a patient and understanding demeanor.

8. Traditional Values:

- Rooted in traditional values, a Capricorn man often appreciates a committed and monogamous relationship. He values loyalty and expects the same from his partner.

9. Responsible and Protective:

- The sense of responsibility extends to the well-being of his partner. A Capricorn man is likely to take on the role of a protector, ensuring the safety and happiness of his loved ones.

10. Challenges in Communication:

- Capricorn men may struggle with expressing their emotions openly. They may find it challenging to communicate their feelings, requiring patience and understanding from their partner.

Tips for a Successful Relationship with a Capricorn Man:

1. Encourage Open Communication: Foster an environment where the Capricorn man feels comfortable expressing his thoughts and feelings.

2. Acknowledge Achievements: Celebrate each other's achievements and successes, reinforcing a sense of mutual support and appreciation.

3. Respect His Need for Independence: Capricorn men value their independence. Allow space for personal pursuits and growth alongside the relationship.

4. Build Trust: Trust is fundamental for a Capricorn man. Be honest, reliable, and consistent to strengthen the foundation of the relationship.

5. Balance Work and Personal Life: Understand and appreciate the importance of finding a balance between work commitments and personal time for a harmonious relationship.

In summary, the Capricorn man brings dedication, stability, and a traditional approach to relationships. While communication and emotional expression may pose challenges, a patient and understanding partner can build a strong and lasting connection with this reliable and committed individual.

Can You Trust Your Capricorn Man

Trusting a Capricorn man involves understanding his personality traits, values, and approach to relationships. While individual characteristics may vary, here are key aspects to consider when it comes to trusting a Capricorn man:

1. Reliability:

- Capricorn men are known for their reliability. They take commitments seriously and strive to fulfill their responsibilities. If a Capricorn man gives his word, he is likely to follow through.

2. Commitment:

- Commitment is a cornerstone of a Capricorn man's approach to relationships. When he decides to be with someone, he tends to be dedicated and loyal, seeking a long-term connection.

3. Traditional Values:

- Capricorn men often adhere to traditional values, including loyalty and fidelity. They value the stability and security that come with committed relationships.

4. Responsible Nature:

- Responsibility is a key trait. Capricorn men take on the role of protectors and providers, ensuring the well-being of their loved ones. This sense of responsibility can contribute to trustworthiness.

5. Work-Life Balance:

- While they are dedicated to their careers, Capricorn men understand the importance of balancing work and personal life. Finding this balance is crucial for a harmonious relationship.

6. Conservative Approach:

- Capricorn men often have a more conservative approach to relationships. They appreciate stability and may not be prone to impulsive actions that could jeopardize trust.

7. Communication Challenges:

- Capricorn men may struggle with expressing their emotions openly. While this can pose challenges in communication, it doesn't necessarily indicate untrustworthiness. Patience and understanding are key.

**8. Need for Independence:

- Capricorn men value their independence. Trusting a Capricorn man involves respecting his need for personal space and allowing room for individual pursuits.

Tips for Building and Maintaining Trust:

1. Encourage Open Communication: Foster an environment where both partners feel comfortable expressing thoughts and feelings openly.

2. Be Reliable: Demonstrate reliability and consistency in your actions. Capricorn men appreciate dependability and may reciprocate with trust.

3. Acknowledge Achievements: Celebrate each other's achievements and successes. Recognizing and supporting each other's goals can strengthen the bond of trust.

4. Understand His Ambitions: Capricorn men are often ambitious. Understanding and supporting their career goals can contribute to trust, as they value a partner who encourages their success.

5. Be Patient: Building trust takes time. Patience is crucial, especially when dealing with a Capricorn man who may take time to open up emotionally.

While trust is an essential aspect of any relationship, it's important to recognize that trust is a mutual effort. Both partners contribute to creating a foundation of trust by being honest, reliable, and understanding of each other's needs and boundaries.

Dating Capricorn Men

Dating a Capricorn man can be a rewarding experience, but understanding his personality traits and preferences is key to building a successful relationship. Here's a guide to navigating the world of dating with a Capricorn man:

1. Understand His Ambitions:

- Capricorn men are ambitious and career-focused. Understand and support his goals, as he values a partner who encourages his success.

2. Be Patient:

- Patience is crucial when dating a Capricorn man. He may take time to open up emotionally, so allow the relationship to develop gradually.

3. Respect His Independence:

- Capricorn men value their independence. Respect his need for personal space and individual pursuits alongside the relationship.

4. Appreciate Stability:

- Stability is important for Capricorn men. Show that you appreciate a committed and stable relationship, as they are often attracted to partners who share this value.

5. Celebrate Achievements:

- Acknowledge and celebrate each other's achievements. Capricorn men appreciate partners who recognize and support their successes.

6. Quality Over Quantity:

- Capricorn men value quality over quantity in relationships. Focus on building a deep and meaningful connection rather than rushing into things.

7. Engage in Intellectual Conversations:

- Capricorn men appreciate intellectual conversations. Engage in discussions about meaningful topics to stimulate his mind and showcase compatibility.

8. Plan Thoughtful Dates:

- Thoughtful and well-planned dates resonate with a Capricorn man. Consider activities that align with his interests and show that you've put thought into the date.

9. Respect Tradition:

- Capricorn men often appreciate tradition. Show respect for traditional values, as this can create a strong foundation for the relationship.

10. Be Supportive:

- Be a supportive partner. Encourage his ambitions, offer a listening ear, and provide emotional support when needed.

Challenges to Be Aware Of:

1. Reserved Nature: Capricorn men can be reserved, making it challenging to express emotions openly. Be patient and understanding as he navigates this aspect.

2. Workaholic Tendencies: Due to their ambitious nature, Capricorn men may become absorbed in their work. Encourage a balance between work and personal life.

3. Fear of Failure: Capricorn men may struggle with a fear of failure, impacting their willingness to take risks in love. Encourage them to embrace vulnerability.

Keeping the Relationship Strong:

1. Celebrate Milestones: Acknowledge and celebrate relationship milestones. Capricorn men appreciate the recognition of shared accomplishments.

2. Communication: Foster open communication about feelings and expectations. Creating a safe space for vulnerability strengthens the bond.

3. Balance: Help the Capricorn man find a balance between work and personal life. Encouraging relaxation and quality time together is essential.

4. Respect Boundaries: Respect his need for personal space and independence. Understanding and appreciating his boundaries contributes to a healthy relationship.

Dating a Capricorn man requires patience, understanding, and a willingness to embrace both the strengths and challenges of his personality. Building a strong foundation rooted in respect and shared values can lead to a fulfilling and lasting relationship.

Understanding Capricorn Men

Understanding Capricorn men involves delving into their personality traits, values, and approach to life. Here's a comprehensive guide to help you gain insight into the world of Capricorn men:

1. Ambitious and Goal-Oriented:

- Capricorn men are driven by ambition. They set high goals for themselves, whether in their careers or personal lives, and work diligently to achieve them.

2. Disciplined and Organized:

- Known for their disciplined approach, Capricorn men thrive in structured environments. They are organized individuals who value order and efficiency.

3. Patient and Persistent:

- Patience is a virtue for Capricorn men. They understand the importance of time and are willing to persistently work toward their objectives, even if it takes a considerable amount of time.

4. Responsible and Reliable:

- Responsibility is a key trait. Capricorn men take their duties seriously, both in their professional and personal lives. They are reliable individuals who can be counted on.

5. Reserved and Cautious:

- Capricorn men can be reserved, especially when it comes to expressing their emotions. They approach relationships and decisions with caution, carefully weighing the pros and cons.

6. Traditional Values:

- Rooted in traditional values, Capricorn men appreciate stability, commitment, and loyalty in relationships. They tend to value long-term connections and may be drawn to traditional roles.

7. Appreciation for Quality:

- Quality matters to Capricorn men in all aspects of life. They appreciate high standards and are attracted to partners, experiences, and possessions that reflect quality.

8. Independent Nature:

- Capricorn men value their independence. While they are committed partners, they also appreciate having personal space to pursue their own interests and goals.

9. Fear of Failure:

- Capricorn men may harbor a fear of failure. This fear can drive them to work exceptionally hard, but it may also make them cautious in taking risks, both in their personal and professional lives.

10. Work-Life Balance:

- Balancing work and personal life is important for Capricorn men. While they are dedicated to their careers, they understand the significance of maintaining a healthy work-life balance.

Challenges in Understanding Capricorn Men:

1. Reserved Expression of Emotions:

- Capricorn men may struggle with expressing their emotions openly. This reserved nature can sometimes make it challenging to understand their feelings.

2. Workaholic Tendencies:

- Due to their ambitious nature, Capricorn men may become absorbed in their work. This workaholic tendency can impact their availability for personal and leisure activities.

3. Difficulty Taking Risks:

- The fear of failure may hinder Capricorn men from taking risks, both emotionally and in pursuing new opportunities. Encouraging them to step out of their comfort zones can be a delicate process.

Tips for Understanding and Building Connections:

1. Encourage Communication: Foster open communication and create a safe space for the Capricorn man to express his thoughts and feelings.

2. Appreciate Quality Time:
Understand that Capricorn men value quality time in relationships. Thoughtful gestures and spending time together contribute to building a strong connection.

3. Celebrate Achievements: Acknowledge and celebrate his achievements. Capricorn men appreciate recognition for their hard work and dedication.

4. Support Independence: Respect his need for independence and support his pursuit of personal goals alongside the relationship.

5. Be Patient: Patience is key when understanding Capricorn men. Allow them the time they need to open up and share their emotions.

By embracing and appreciating the unique qualities of Capricorn men, you can build a strong and meaningful connection based on mutual respect and understanding.

Capricorn Man Likes And Dislikes

Understanding the likes and dislikes of a Capricorn man can provide valuable insights into his preferences and personality. Keep in mind that individual preferences may vary, but here are some general traits associated with Capricorn men:

Likes:

1. Ambition and Success:

- Capricorn men are drawn to ambition and success, both in themselves and in their partners. They appreciate individuals who are goal-oriented and driven.

2. Quality and Class:

- Quality matters to Capricorn men. They have a refined taste and appreciate well-made, high-quality items, whether in fashion, home decor, or other aspects of life.

3. Tradition and Stability:

- Rooted in traditional values, Capricorn men appreciate stability and commitment in relationships. They are drawn to partners who share a similar commitment to long-term connections.

4. **Hard Work and Dedication:**

- Capricorn men value hard work and dedication. They respect individuals who put in the effort to achieve their goals and appreciate the same level of commitment in their partners.

5. **Intelligence and Wit:**

- Capricorn men are attracted to intelligence and wit. Engaging in intellectual conversations and showcasing a sharp mind can capture their interest.

6. **Patience and Persistence:**

- Patience is a virtue appreciated by Capricorn men. They value individuals who can persistently work toward their goals and remain patient in the face of challenges.

7. **Well-Planned and Thoughtful Gestures:**

- Capricorn men appreciate well-planned and thoughtful gestures. Whether it's a carefully planned date or a meaningful gift, they value the effort put into creating memorable experiences.

8. **Responsibility and Reliability:**

- Responsibility is a key trait for Capricorn men. They appreciate individuals who are reliable, trustworthy, and take their commitments seriously.

Dislikes:

1. **Impulsiveness:**

- Capricorn men may dislike impulsiveness, especially when it comes to major decisions or actions. They prefer well-thought-out plans and actions.

2. **Disorganization and Chaos:**

- Given their organized nature, Capricorn men may be put off by disorganization and chaos. They appreciate order and structure in their surroundings.

3. **Lack of Ambition:**

- A lack of ambition or drive can be a turn-off for Capricorn men. They are attracted to individuals who have clear goals and aspirations.

4. **Unreliability:**

- Capricorn men value reliability. Being unreliable or failing to fulfill commitments can be a source of frustration for them.

5. **Overly Emotional Behavior:**

- Capricorn men, being reserved themselves, may find overly emotional behavior uncomfortable. They appreciate a balanced and measured approach to emotions.

6. **Lack of Patience:**

- Impatience may be a point of contention for Capricorn men. They appreciate individuals who can approach challenges with patience and persistence.

7. **Recklessness:**

- Capricorn men may dislike recklessness, whether in financial matters or personal choices. They prefer calculated risks and responsible decision-making.

Understanding a Capricorn man's likes and dislikes provides valuable insights for building a harmonious relationship. It's essential to communicate openly and find common ground while respecting each other's individual preferences.

How To Choose A Gift For Your Capricorn Man

Choosing a gift for a Capricorn man involves considering his personality traits, preferences, and interests. Here are some tips to help you select a thoughtful and meaningful gift for your Capricorn man:

1. Practical Gifts:

- Capricorn men appreciate practicality. Consider giving him a gift that serves a useful purpose or aligns with his daily activities. This could be a high-quality leather wallet, a well-crafted briefcase, or a practical gadget.

2. Quality Over Quantity:

- Capricorn men value quality over quantity. Choose a gift that reflects craftsmanship and durability. Opt for items made from premium materials, whether it's a piece of clothing, accessories, or gadgets.

3. Traditional and Classic Items:

- Capricorn men often appreciate traditional and classic items. Consider gifts with timeless appeal, such as a classic watch, a well-tailored suit, or a sophisticated piece of jewelry.

4. Thoughtful Gestures:

- Show your thoughtfulness through gestures. Plan a well-thought-out date or experience that aligns with his interests. It could be a weekend getaway, a visit to a museum, or tickets to a concert or show.

5. Ambition-Related Gifts:

- Consider gifts that align with his ambitions and goals. This could be a book by a successful entrepreneur, a motivational journal, or an item related to his career or hobbies.

6. Tech Gadgets:

- Capricorn men often appreciate practical and functional tech gadgets. Consider items like the latest smartwatch, noise-canceling headphones, or a versatile tablet that can aid in both work and leisure.

7. Subscription Services:

- If he has specific interests, consider subscription services related to those interests. It could be a subscription to a magazine, a streaming service for his favorite shows or movies, or a monthly delivery of gourmet snacks or coffee.

8. Personalized Items:

- Personalized gifts show that you've put thought into the present. Consider personalized items like engraved cufflinks, a monogrammed leather portfolio, or custom-made artwork.

9. Home Decor:

- Choose sophisticated and timeless home decor items that complement his style. This could be a high-quality set of whiskey glasses, a classic piece of artwork, or elegant decor for his workspace.

10. Books or Educational Material:

- Capricorn men often appreciate expanding their knowledge. Consider gifting him a book by his favorite author, a course or workshop related to his interests, or educational material that aligns with his goals.

11. Fitness Gear:

- If he is health-conscious or enjoys staying fit, consider fitness-related gifts such as quality workout gear, a fitness tracker, or a gym bag.

Remember:

- Pay attention to his interests and hobbies.

- Consider his personal style and preferences.

- Opt for gifts that align with his goals and ambitions.

- Quality, thoughtfulness, and practicality are key considerations.

By choosing a gift that reflects his personality and interests, you can show your Capricorn man that you've put thought into the present, making it more meaningful and appreciated.

Capricorn Woman: The Ultimate Guide

Capricorn Woman: The Ultimate Guide

The Capricorn woman is a force to be reckoned with, blending ambition, practicality, and a strong sense of responsibility. This ultimate guide provides an in-depth exploration of the Capricorn woman's characteristics, personality traits, and key aspects of her life.

Personality Traits:

1. **Ambitious and Driven:**

- The Capricorn woman is highly ambitious, with a clear vision of her goals. She strives for success in her personal and professional life.

2. **Practical and Grounded:**

- Grounded in reality, she approaches life with a practical mindset. The Capricorn woman values stability and takes a realistic approach to challenges.

3. **Responsible and Reliable:**

- Responsibility is a cornerstone of her character. She is reliable and can be counted on to fulfill her commitments, both in relationships and work.

4. **Disciplined and Organized:**

- Known for her discipline, the Capricorn woman thrives in organized environments. She appreciates order and efficiency in her daily life.

5. **Independent and Self-Sufficient:**

- Independence is a key trait. The Capricorn woman values self-sufficiency and is capable of managing her affairs with competence.

6. **Reserved and Cautious:**

- Cautious in her approach, the Capricorn woman takes her time to assess situations and relationships. She may be reserved when it comes to expressing emotions openly.

7. **Traditional Values:**

- Rooted in traditional values, she appreciates stability, commitment, and loyalty in relationships. The Capricorn woman often values long-term connections.

8. Sophisticated and Classy:

- The Capricorn woman has a sophisticated and classy demeanor. She appreciates quality in all aspects of life, from fashion to home decor.

Love and Relationships:

1. Serious About Commitment:

- In love, the Capricorn woman is serious about commitment. She seeks a partner who shares her values and is ready for a long-term, stable relationship.

2. Demonstrates Love Through Actions:

- While not overly expressive verbally, she demonstrates her love through practical gestures and acts of service. Actions speak louder than words for the Capricorn woman.

3. Balances Work and Personal Life:

- Maintaining a balance between work and personal life is crucial. The Capricorn woman understands the importance of nurturing her relationships alongside her professional pursuits.

4. Values Loyalty and Trust:

- Loyalty is paramount for the Capricorn woman. She values trust and expects the same level of commitment and faithfulness from her partner.

5. Traditional Romance:

- She appreciates traditional expressions of romance. Thoughtful gestures, classic dates, and meaningful gifts resonate with the Capricorn woman.

Career and Ambitions:

1. Driven Toward Success:

- The Capricorn woman is driven toward success in her career. She sets high standards and works diligently to achieve her professional goals.

2. Methodical and Strategic:

- A methodical approach characterizes her work style. She plans and strategizes, ensuring that every step aligns with her long-term objectives.

3. **Leadership Qualities:**

- Natural leadership qualities often propel the Capricorn woman into positions of authority. She is capable of managing and inspiring others with her strong work ethic.

4. **Financial Savvy:**

- Financial stability is important. The Capricorn woman is often financially savvy, making prudent decisions to secure her future.

5. **Balances Professional and Personal Life:**

- While dedicated to her career, she understands the significance of balancing professional success with a fulfilling personal life.

Challenges and Growth Areas:

1. **Difficulty Expressing Emotions:**

- The reserved nature of the Capricorn woman may lead to challenges in expressing emotions openly. Communicating feelings can be an area for growth.

2. Struggles with Delegating:

- Due to her independent nature, she may struggle with delegating tasks. Learning to trust others with responsibilities can contribute to personal and professional growth.

3. Fear of Vulnerability:

- A fear of vulnerability might hinder deep emotional connections. Overcoming this fear and embracing vulnerability can enhance personal relationships.

Health and Wellness:

1. Stress Management is Crucial:

- Given her ambitious nature, stress management is crucial. The Capricorn woman benefits from incorporating relaxation techniques into her routine.

2. Prioritizes Physical Health:

- Physical health is a priority. Regular exercise, a balanced diet, and sufficient rest contribute to her overall well-being.

3. **Mindfulness and Reflection:**

- Incorporating mindfulness practices and self-reflection helps the Capricorn woman maintain mental and emotional balance.

Friendship and Social Life:

1. **Selectively Social:**

- The Capricorn woman is selectively social. While she values quality friendships, she may not have an extensive social circle.

2. **Loyal and Supportive Friend:**

- Loyal to those she cares about, the Capricorn woman is a supportive friend. She values deep connections and is there for her friends in times of need.

Fashion and Style:

1. **Classic and Timeless Fashion:**

- Capricorn women often have a classic and timeless fashion sense. They appreciate well-tailored, high-quality pieces that exude sophistication.

2. **Understated Elegance:**

- Understated elegance characterizes her style. She opts for refined, classy pieces that make a statement without being overly flamboyant.

Conclusion:

The Capricorn woman is a powerhouse of ambition, resilience, and traditional values. Balancing her professional and personal life with grace, she seeks stability and commitment in relationships. This ultimate guide provides a comprehensive understanding of the Capricorn woman's multifaceted personality, offering insights into her love life, career, challenges, and more.

Capricorn Woman In Love

The Capricorn woman in love is a complex blend of practicality, loyalty, and a deep sense of commitment. Understanding how she approaches romantic relationships provides insights into her behavior, preferences, and the dynamics of her love life.

1. Serious and Committed:

- When a Capricorn woman enters a romantic relationship, she takes it seriously. Commitment is a cornerstone of her approach to love, and she seeks a partner who shares her dedication to a long-lasting, stable connection.

2. Demonstrates Love Through Actions:

- The Capricorn woman may not express her emotions with grand gestures or excessive words of affection. Instead, she demonstrates her love through practical actions and acts of service. She believes in the power of showing love through meaningful deeds.

3. Reserved Expression of Emotions:

- Capricorn women tend to be reserved when it comes to expressing their emotions openly. This reserved nature can sometimes be mistaken for a lack of affection, but it's essential to understand that she values depth and authenticity in emotional expression.

4. Balances Work and Love:

- Maintaining a balance between her professional and personal life is crucial for the Capricorn woman. While she is committed to her career, she understands the importance of nurturing her romantic relationship and creating a harmonious blend between the two.

5. Traditional Romance:

- The Capricorn woman appreciates traditional expressions of romance. Classic dates, thoughtful gestures, and meaningful gifts resonate with her. She values the timeless aspects of love and may not be drawn to overly extravagant or flashy displays of affection.

6. Loyalty and Trust:

- Loyalty is of utmost importance to the Capricorn woman in love. She expects her partner to be trustworthy and committed, and she reciprocates with unwavering loyalty. Building a foundation of trust is crucial for the success of her relationships.

7. Building a Future Together:

- Capricorn women often approach love with a long-term perspective. They seek partners with whom they can build a stable and secure future. Discussions about shared goals, plans, and aspirations are meaningful and appreciated.

8. Practical Considerations:

- Practicality plays a significant role in the Capricorn woman's approach to love. She considers the practical aspects of a relationship, such as financial stability, shared responsibilities, and the ability to navigate life's challenges together.

9. Expressing Vulnerability:

- While Capricorn women may be reserved, they appreciate partners with whom they can feel safe expressing vulnerability. Building a strong emotional connection involves creating an environment where she feels comfortable sharing her feelings.

10. Support and Encouragement: - In love, the Capricorn woman values a supportive and encouraging partner. She appreciates someone who understands her ambitions and provides the necessary support to help her achieve her goals.

Challenges in Love:

1. Difficulty Expressing Emotions:

- The reserved nature of the Capricorn woman may lead to challenges in expressing emotions openly. Encouraging open communication and creating a safe space for emotional expression can help overcome this hurdle.

2. Work-Life Balance:

- Balancing her career and love life can be a challenge. It's important for the Capricorn woman to find a harmonious equilibrium between her professional ambitions and the nurturing of her romantic relationship.

3. Fear of Vulnerability:

- A fear of vulnerability might hinder deep emotional connections. Encouraging her to embrace vulnerability and express her feelings openly can foster a stronger emotional bond.

Tips for Loving a Capricorn Woman:

1. Show Appreciation for Practical Gestures:

- Appreciate the practical ways she shows love, whether through acts of service or thoughtful gestures that contribute to the stability of the relationship.

2. Demonstrate Reliability and Trustworthiness:

- Build trust by demonstrating reliability and trustworthiness. Consistency in actions and words helps strengthen the foundation of the relationship.

3. **Engage in Meaningful Conversations:**

- Engage in conversations about shared goals, plans for the future, and other meaningful aspects of life. The Capricorn woman values a partner who is willing to discuss the practical considerations of the relationship.

4. **Support Her Ambitions:**

- Support her professional ambitions and personal goals. Understanding and encouraging her career aspirations is a key way to show love and partnership.

5. **Create a Balanced and Harmonious Environment:**

- Help create a balanced environment where she can thrive both in her career and personal life. Finding ways to harmonize work and love contributes to her overall well-being.

In conclusion, the Capricorn woman in love brings a unique combination of dedication, practicality, and loyalty to her relationships. Understanding her reserved nature, valuing her practical expressions of love, and supporting her in both her career and personal aspirations are essential for a successful and fulfilling connection with this grounded and ambitious individual.

Capricorn Woman Sexuality

The sexuality of a Capricorn woman is characterized by a blend of sensuality, practicality, and a deep connection to her emotional and physical well-being. Understanding her sexual nature involves recognizing the traits and preferences that contribute to her intimate relationships.

1. Reserved and Private:

- Capricorn women are often reserved and private, including in matters of sexuality. They value intimacy as a personal and meaningful aspect of their relationships, keeping these experiences within the confines of trust and emotional connection.

2. Deep Emotional Connection:

- For a Capricorn woman, a deep emotional connection is a crucial foundation for a satisfying sexual relationship. Trust, loyalty, and a sense of security contribute to her ability to fully express her sexuality with a partner.

3. Practical Approach to Intimacy:

- Practicality extends to the bedroom for a Capricorn woman. She approaches intimacy with a goal-oriented mindset, valuing the physical and emotional benefits that come with a healthy sexual relationship.

4. Loyalty and Commitment:

- Loyalty and commitment play a significant role in the sexual dynamics of a Capricorn woman. She seeks a partner with whom she can build a long-lasting and committed bond, enhancing the depth of their intimate connection.

5. Traditional Values:

- Rooted in traditional values, Capricorn women often appreciate a sense of tradition and stability in their sexual relationships. Routine and familiarity can contribute to a sense of security, allowing her to fully express her desires.

6. Expressing Sensuality:

- Capricorn women may express sensuality in a subtle and refined manner. Their approach to physical affection is often elegant, and they appreciate partners who can match their level of sophistication.

7. Appreciation for Quality:

- Quality matters in all aspects of a Capricorn woman's life, including her intimate relationships. She appreciates a partner who values the finer things in life and is attuned to the importance of creating a comfortable and aesthetically pleasing environment.

8. Building Trust and Comfort:

- Building trust and comfort is essential for a Capricorn woman to fully embrace her sexuality. She needs to feel secure in the relationship to express herself authentically and explore the depths of intimacy with her partner.

9. Balancing Work and Intimacy:

- Balancing work and intimacy is a consideration for a Capricorn woman. Creating a harmonious equilibrium between her professional life and her personal relationships contributes to her overall well-being and ability to engage in a satisfying sexual connection.

10. Communication is Key: - Communication is vital in the sexual relationships of a Capricorn woman. While she may be reserved, expressing desires, boundaries, and preferences openly helps create a mutually satisfying and fulfilling intimate connection.

Challenges in Sexuality:

1. Difficulty Expressing Fantasies:

- Capricorn women may find it challenging to express their sexual fantasies openly. Encouraging open communication and creating a non-judgmental space can help overcome barriers and enhance intimacy.

2. Work-Related Stress:

- Work-related stress can impact the sexual life of a Capricorn woman. It's essential to find ways to manage stress and create a supportive environment that allows her to relax and enjoy intimate moments.

3. Fear of Vulnerability:

- A fear of vulnerability may hinder the exploration of deeper emotional and sexual connections. Encouraging a sense of security and trust is crucial for overcoming this fear.

Tips for Enhancing Intimacy:

1. **Prioritize Emotional Connection:**

- Prioritize building and maintaining a deep emotional connection with your Capricorn partner. Emotional intimacy enhances the overall satisfaction of the sexual relationship.

2. **Create a Comfortable Environment:**

- Pay attention to the ambiance and create a comfortable and aesthetically pleasing environment. A Capricorn woman appreciates quality and refinement in all aspects of her life, including the bedroom.

3. **Encourage Open Communication:**

- Foster open communication about desires, boundaries, and preferences. Creating a safe space for discussing intimate matters allows for a more satisfying and harmonious sexual relationship.

4. **Support Work-Life Balance:**

- Support her in achieving a healthy work-life balance. Finding ways to alleviate work-related stress contributes to a more relaxed and enjoyable intimate connection.

5. **Celebrate Tradition and Routine:**

- Embrace elements of tradition and routine that resonate with her. Capricorn women appreciate stability, and incorporating familiar routines into intimate moments can enhance the overall experience.

Understanding the nuanced and reserved nature of a Capricorn woman's sexuality is crucial for creating a fulfilling and lasting intimate connection. By fostering trust, prioritizing emotional intimacy, and appreciating the value of tradition, partners can enhance the depth and satisfaction of the sexual relationship with a Capricorn woman.

Capricorn Woman In Relationships

The Capricorn woman in relationships is a blend of practicality, loyalty, and a deep commitment to building stable and lasting connections. Understanding how she approaches romantic relationships provides insights into her behavior, preferences, and the dynamics of her partnerships.

1. Serious and Committed:

- When a Capricorn woman enters a relationship, she takes it seriously. Commitment is a cornerstone of her approach to love, and she seeks a partner who shares her dedication to a long-lasting, stable connection.

2. Demonstrates Love Through Actions:

- The Capricorn woman may not express her emotions with grand gestures or excessive words of affection. Instead, she demonstrates her love through practical actions and acts of service. She believes in the power of showing love through meaningful deeds.

3. Balances Work and Relationship:

- Maintaining a balance between her professional and personal life is crucial for the Capricorn woman. While she is committed to her career, she understands the importance of nurturing her romantic relationship and creating a harmonious blend between the two.

4. Traditional Romance:

- The Capricorn woman appreciates traditional expressions of romance. Classic dates, thoughtful gestures, and meaningful gifts resonate with her. She values the timeless aspects of love and may not be drawn to overly extravagant or flashy displays of affection.

5. Loyalty and Trust:

- Loyalty is of utmost importance to the Capricorn woman in relationships. She expects her partner to be trustworthy and committed, and she reciprocates with unwavering loyalty. Building a foundation of trust is crucial for the success of her partnerships.

6. Building a Future Together:

- Capricorn women often approach relationships with a long-term perspective. They seek partners with whom they can build a stable and secure future. Discussions about shared goals, plans, and aspirations are meaningful and appreciated.

7. Practical Considerations:

- Practicality plays a significant role in the Capricorn woman's approach to relationships. She considers the practical aspects of a partnership, such as financial stability, shared responsibilities, and the ability to navigate life's challenges together.

8. Expressing Vulnerability:

- While Capricorn women may be reserved, they appreciate partners with whom they can feel safe expressing vulnerability. Building a strong emotional connection involves creating an environment where she feels comfortable sharing her feelings.

9. Support and Encouragement:

- In relationships, the Capricorn woman values a supportive and encouraging partner. She appreciates someone who understands her ambitions and provides the necessary support to help her achieve her goals.

Challenges in Relationships:

1. **Difficulty Expressing Emotions:**

- The reserved nature of the Capricorn woman may lead to challenges in expressing emotions openly. Encouraging open communication and creating a safe space for emotional expression can help overcome this hurdle.

2. **Work-Life Balance:**

- Balancing her career and love life can be a challenge. It's important for the Capricorn woman to find a harmonious equilibrium between her professional ambitions and the nurturing of her romantic relationship.

3. **Fear of Vulnerability:**

- A fear of vulnerability might hinder deep emotional connections. Encouraging her to embrace vulnerability and express her feelings openly can foster a stronger emotional bond.

Tips for a Successful Relationship with a Capricorn Woman:

1. Show Appreciation for Practical Gestures:

- Appreciate the practical ways she shows love, whether through acts of service or thoughtful gestures that contribute to the stability of the relationship.

2. Demonstrate Reliability and Trustworthiness:

- Build trust by demonstrating reliability and trustworthiness. Consistency in actions and words helps strengthen the foundation of the relationship.

3. Engage in Meaningful Conversations:

- Engage in conversations about shared goals, plans for the future, and other meaningful aspects of life. The Capricorn woman values a partner who is willing to discuss the practical considerations of the relationship.

4. Support Her Ambitions:

- Support her professional ambitions and personal goals. Understanding and encouraging her career aspirations is a key way to show love and partnership.

5. Create a Balanced and Harmonious Environment:

- Help create a balanced environment where she can thrive both in her career and personal life. Finding ways to harmonize work and love contributes to her overall well-being.

In conclusion, the Capricorn woman in relationships brings a unique combination of dedication, practicality, and loyalty to her partnerships. Understanding her reserved nature, valuing her practical expressions of love, and supporting her in both her career and personal aspirations are essential for a successful and fulfilling connection with this grounded and ambitious individual.

Can You Trust Your Capricorn Woman

Trust is a fundamental aspect of any healthy relationship, and the trustworthiness of a Capricorn woman is influenced by her character traits and values. Understanding key aspects of her personality can provide insights into whether you can trust your Capricorn woman.

1. Loyalty is Paramount:

- Capricorn women place a high value on loyalty. Once committed to a relationship, they tend to be faithful and dedicated partners. Trust is built on the foundation of loyalty, and a Capricorn woman is likely to prioritize the security of the relationship.

2. Consistency and Reliability:

- Trust is reinforced through consistency and reliability. Capricorn women often demonstrate trustworthiness by being consistent in their actions and reliable in fulfilling commitments. They appreciate these qualities in others as well.

3. Practical Approach to Trust:

- Capricorn women have a practical approach to trust. They assess situations based on facts and actions rather than solely relying on emotions. Trust is earned through observable behavior and reliability.

4. Open Communication:

- Capricorn women value open and honest communication. If there are concerns or issues, they prefer addressing them directly and finding practical solutions. Establishing clear lines of communication contributes to building trust in the relationship.

5. Building a Stable Foundation:

- Trust is crucial for Capricorn women when it comes to building a stable and secure foundation in a relationship. They seek partners who share their values and are committed to creating a trustworthy and reliable partnership.

6. Reluctance to Risk Betrayal:

- Capricorn women are generally cautious and reluctant to risk betrayal. They take the time to observe and assess before fully opening up. Once trust is established, they can be deeply committed and reliable partners.

7. Professional Integrity:

- Capricorn women often exhibit a strong sense of professional integrity, and this can extend to their personal lives. Trustworthiness in professional matters can translate into a reliable and trustworthy approach in personal relationships.

8. Conservative Approach to Relationships:

- Capricorn women tend to take a conservative approach to relationships. They don't engage in impulsive actions that could jeopardize trust. Instead, they focus on building a solid foundation based on shared values and commitment.

Challenges to Trust:

1. **Difficulty Expressing Emotions:**

- Capricorn women may find it challenging to express their emotions openly. This reserved nature can create moments of uncertainty, but it's important to recognize that they demonstrate trust through actions and reliability.

2. Cautious in New Relationships:

- In the early stages of a relationship, a Capricorn woman may be cautious and take time to build trust. Patience is key, as rushing or pressuring her may create challenges in establishing a strong foundation of trust.

3. Work-Life Balance:

- Balancing work and personal life can sometimes pose challenges. If a Capricorn woman is heavily focused on her career, it's important to find a balance that ensures both professional and personal commitments are met.

Tips for Building and Maintaining Trust:

1. Demonstrate Reliability:

- Consistent and reliable behavior is key to earning and maintaining the trust of a Capricorn woman. Fulfilling commitments and being dependable contribute to building a strong foundation of trust.

2. Open Communication:

- Foster open and honest communication. Discussing concerns, feelings, and expectations directly helps create a transparent environment that supports trust in the relationship.

3. Respect Boundaries:

- Respect the boundaries of a Capricorn woman and avoid pressuring her to open up quickly. Allow her the time and space to build trust at her own pace.

4. Show Loyalty:

- Demonstrate loyalty and commitment to the relationship. Capricorn women value partners who prioritize the security and stability of the connection.

5. Be Patient:

- Patience is crucial in building trust with a Capricorn woman. Trust is established over time, and rushing the process can create unnecessary challenges.

In conclusion, trusting a Capricorn woman is often based on her values of loyalty, consistency, and practicality. By demonstrating reliability, fostering open communication, and respecting boundaries, you can build a strong foundation of trust in your relationship with a Capricorn woman.

Dating Capricorn Woman

Dating a Capricorn woman requires an understanding of her personality traits, values, and approach to relationships. Capricorn women are known for their practicality, ambition, and commitment, and navigating the dating process with them involves being mindful of these characteristics. Here are some tips for dating a Capricorn woman:

1. Show Ambition and Drive:

- Capricorn women are ambitious and driven individuals. Demonstrate your own ambitions and goals, and show that you have a sense of direction in your life. They appreciate partners who share their commitment to personal and professional growth.

2. Plan Thoughtful and Practical Dates:

- Capricorn women appreciate thoughtful and practical dates. Plan activities that align with their interests and preferences. Whether it's a cozy dinner, a cultural outing, or a nature walk, choose activities that allow for meaningful conversation and connection.

3. Be Patient and Respectful:

- Capricorn women can be cautious in the early stages of a relationship. Be patient and respectful of their pace. Avoid pressuring them into opening up too quickly and allow the relationship to develop organically.

4. Express Your Intentions Clearly:

- Capricorn women value honesty and directness. Express your intentions and feelings clearly. They appreciate partners who communicate openly and transparently about their expectations in the relationship.

5. Be Reliable and Consistent:

- Reliability is key when dating a Capricorn woman. Be consistent in your actions and commitments. Showing that you can be depended upon builds trust and contributes to the stability of the relationship.

6. Respect Her Independence:

- Capricorn women value their independence. Respect their need for personal space and autonomy. A healthy balance between shared time and individual pursuits is important in a relationship with a Capricorn woman.

7. Engage in Meaningful Conversations:

- Capricorn women appreciate meaningful conversations. Discuss topics that go beyond surface-level discussions and delve into shared values, aspirations, and life goals. Engaging in intellectually stimulating conversations strengthens the connection.

8. Demonstrate Financial Responsibility:

- Capricorn women are often financially responsible and value stability. Show that you have a practical approach to financial matters and are responsible in managing your resources. Financial stability is a significant consideration for them.

9. Celebrate Tradition:

- Capricorn women often appreciate traditional values. Consider incorporating elements of tradition into your dating experiences. Whether it's celebrating special occasions or embracing timeless gestures of romance, these traditions resonate with them.

10. Support Her Career Goals: - Career is important to Capricorn women, and they appreciate partners who support their professional ambitions. Show interest in and support for her career goals, and understand the importance she places on achieving success in her endeavors.

Challenges in Dating a Capricorn Woman:

1. **Reserved Nature:**

- Capricorn women can be reserved, making it challenging to gauge their emotions early in the dating process. Patience and a willingness to build trust over time are essential.

2. **Cautious Approach:**

- They may take a cautious approach to relationships, evaluating compatibility and trust before fully opening up. This cautiousness can extend the duration of the dating phase.

3. Balancing Work and Personal Life:

- Balancing work commitments with personal life can be a challenge. Understanding and supporting her need to manage both aspects of her life is important for a successful relationship.

Tips for Dating Success:

1. Be Patient:

- Patience is key when dating a Capricorn woman. Allow the relationship to develop naturally and respect her timeline for emotional connection.

2. Show Appreciation for Practical Gestures:

- Appreciate the practical ways she may express affection, whether through acts of service or thoughtful gestures that contribute to the stability of the relationship.

3. Celebrate Achievements:

- Celebrate her achievements and milestones, both in her personal life and career. Acknowledging her successes demonstrates your support and encouragement.

4. Communicate Openly:

- Foster open communication about expectations, desires, and boundaries. A Capricorn woman values partners who communicate openly and transparently.

5. Plan for the Future:

- Discuss shared goals and plans for the future. Capricorn women appreciate partners who share a long-term vision and are committed to building a stable and secure future together.

Dating a Capricorn woman can be a rewarding experience when approached with understanding, patience, and a genuine commitment to building a strong foundation for a lasting relationship.

Understanding Your Capricorn Woman

Understanding a Capricorn woman involves recognizing her personality traits, values, and the way she navigates various aspects of life, including relationships. Capricorn women are known for their practicality, ambition, and commitment. Here are key aspects to consider when seeking to understand your Capricorn woman:

1. Practical and Goal-Oriented:

- Capricorn women approach life with practicality and a goal-oriented mindset. They are driven to achieve their ambitions and appreciate partners who share a sense of direction in life. Understanding her goals and supporting her aspirations is essential.

2. Reserved Nature:

- Capricorn women can be reserved, especially in the early stages of a relationship. They may take time to open up emotionally. Be patient and create an environment where she feels comfortable expressing her feelings at her own pace.

3. Ambitious and Career-Focused:

- Career success is often a significant priority for Capricorn women. They are ambitious and value partners who understand

and support their professional goals. Acknowledge and encourage her aspirations in both her personal and professional life.

4. Loyalty and Commitment:

- Loyalty is paramount for Capricorn women. Once committed to a relationship, they are likely to be faithful and dedicated partners. Understand the importance of loyalty in building trust and stability in your connection.

5. Balancing Work and Personal Life:

- Balancing work commitments with personal life can be a challenge for Capricorn women. Understanding and supporting her need to manage both aspects of her life is crucial. Discussing ways to achieve a harmonious balance contributes to relationship success.

6. Traditional Values:

- Capricorn women often appreciate traditional values. They may find comfort in rituals, celebrations, and timeless gestures of romance. Embrace elements of tradition in your relationship to align with her preferences.

7. Independent Yet Family-Oriented:

- While Capricorn women value their independence, they are also family-oriented. Balancing personal autonomy with a commitment to family is important to them. Respect her need for space while nurturing a strong connection with family.

8. Practical Expressions of Love:

- Capricorn women may express love in practical ways, such as through acts of service or thoughtful gestures. Appreciate and reciprocate these expressions, as they contribute to the stability and harmony of the relationship.

9. Cautious in Relationships:

- Capricorn women can be cautious in relationships, taking the time to assess compatibility and trust. Understand that their cautious approach is rooted in a desire for a stable and lasting connection.

10. Appreciation for Quality: - Capricorn women appreciate quality in all aspects of life. From the environment they create to the relationships they build, quality matters. Show an appreciation for refinement, and strive for excellence in your shared experiences.

Challenges in Understanding:

1. **Reserved Communication Style:**

- The reserved nature of Capricorn women may pose challenges in understanding their emotions. Encourage open communication and create a safe space for them to express their feelings.

2. **Work-Related Stress:**

- Work-related stress can impact their overall well-being and, consequently, their interactions in relationships. Be supportive during times of stress and work together to find effective coping mechanisms.

3. **Balancing Independence and Connection:**

- Balancing the desire for independence with the need for emotional connection may be a nuanced challenge. Respect her autonomy while nurturing a strong emotional bond.

Tips for Understanding Success:

1. Communicate Openly and Honestly:

- Foster open and honest communication. Encourage her to express her thoughts and feelings, and be willing to share your own. Transparency is key to understanding each other.

2. Support Professional Ambitions:

- Support her in achieving her professional ambitions. Understand the importance she places on career success and provide encouragement for her endeavors.

3. Create a Harmonious Environment:

- Work together to create a harmonious environment that accommodates both her career aspirations and personal life. Finding a balance contributes to her overall well-being.

4. **Celebrate Achievements:**

- Celebrate her achievements and milestones, both big and small. Recognizing and acknowledging her successes reinforces your support and understanding.

5. **Respect Her Need for Space:**

- Respect her need for personal space and autonomy. Balancing independence with connection is crucial for a healthy and understanding relationship.

Understanding your Capricorn woman involves recognizing her unique blend of practicality, ambition, and commitment. By appreciating her values, supporting her goals, and fostering open communication, you can build a strong foundation for a lasting and fulfilling connection.

Capricorn Woman Likes And Dislikes

Understanding the likes and dislikes of a Capricorn woman can provide valuable insights into what resonates with her and what aspects of life she may find less appealing. Keep in mind that individual preferences may vary, but here are general tendencies based on the Capricorn woman's personality traits:

Likes:

1. Ambition and Success:

- Capricorn women are drawn to ambition and success. They appreciate individuals who share their drive to achieve goals and pursue excellence in their endeavors.

2. Traditional Values:

- Capricorn women often appreciate traditional values. Rituals, celebrations, and timeless gestures of romance are likely to resonate with them.

3. Quality and Refinement:

- Quality matters to Capricorn women. They appreciate refined experiences, whether in the form of well-crafted items, elegant surroundings, or high standards in various aspects of life.

4. **Practical Expressions of Love:**

- Capricorn women may express and appreciate love through practical gestures and acts of service. Thoughtful actions that contribute to the stability of the relationship are valued.

5. **Reliability and Consistency:**

- Reliability and consistency are important to Capricorn women. They appreciate partners who fulfill commitments and are dependable in their actions.

6. **Intellectual Stimulation:**

- Capricorn women enjoy engaging in meaningful conversations and intellectual stimulation. Discussing topics beyond surface-level discussions contributes to a deep connection.

7. **Professional Achievements:**

- Acknowledging and celebrating professional achievements is significant for Capricorn women. They value partners who understand the importance of career success.

8. **Independence and Autonomy:**

- While valuing relationships, Capricorn women also appreciate their independence and autonomy. They like partners who respect their need for personal space and individual pursuits.

Dislikes:

1. **Impulsiveness:**

- Capricorn women may be cautious and dislike impulsiveness. They prefer well-thought-out decisions and actions over impulsive behavior that can disrupt stability.

2. **Disorganization:**

- Disorganization and chaos may be displeasing to Capricorn women. They prefer order and structure in both their personal and professional lives.

3. **Lack of Ambition:**

- A lack of ambition or a passive approach to life may be a turn-off for Capricorn women. They are attracted to individuals with goals and a drive to succeed.

4. **Unreliability:**

- Unreliable behavior and inconsistency are likely to be disliked. Capricorn women value partners who can be depended upon and fulfill their commitments.

5. **Excessive Emotionality:**

- Capricorn women, with their reserved nature, may find excessive emotionality uncomfortable. They prefer a more practical and composed approach to emotions.

6. **Resistance to Tradition:**

- Resisting or dismissing traditional values may not align well with Capricorn women. They appreciate partners who understand and respect traditional aspects of life.

7. **Lack of Communication:**

- Capricorn women value open communication. A lack of communication or avoidance of meaningful discussions may be a source of frustration for them.

8. **Neglecting Professional Goals:**

- Neglecting or undermining the importance of professional goals can be a point of dissatisfaction for Capricorn women. They value partners who recognize and support their career aspirations.

Understanding a Capricorn woman's likes and dislikes involves appreciating her values, priorities, and the qualities that contribute to stability and success in her life. Building a relationship that aligns with these preferences can lead to a more fulfilling connection.

How To Chose A Gift For Your Capricorn Woman

Choosing a gift for a Capricorn woman involves considering her practical nature, appreciation for quality, and alignment with her ambitions and values. Here are some thoughtful ideas to help you select a gift that resonates with a Capricorn woman:

1. Quality Accessories:

- Consider gifting her high-quality accessories, such as a classic watch, a well-crafted leather handbag, or elegant jewelry. Capricorn women appreciate items that reflect refinement and enduring style.

2. Professional Tools or Equipment:

- If she has a professional or hobby-related interest, consider gifting her tools or equipment that enhance her capabilities. This could include a sophisticated pen, a high-quality planner, or specialized gear related to her interests.

3. Timeless Jewelry:

- Choose timeless jewelry that complements her style. Classic pieces, such as a pearl necklace or a pair of stud earrings, appeal to her appreciation for enduring elegance.

4. Luxurious Skincare or Beauty Products:

- Treat her to luxurious skincare or beauty products that offer a pampering experience. Opt for high-quality brands known for their effectiveness and indulgence.

5. Practical Gadgets:

- Capricorn women often appreciate practical gadgets that make their daily lives more efficient. Consider items like a smartwatch, a high-tech kitchen appliance, or a versatile electronic device.

6. Customized Professional Items:

- Personalized or customized professional items can be meaningful. This could include a monogrammed leather portfolio, a customized business card holder, or a personalized desk accessory.

7. Artisanal or Handcrafted Items:

- Choose artisanal or handcrafted items that showcase craftsmanship and attention to detail. This could be a handwoven scarf, a custom piece of pottery, or artisanal chocolates.

8. Books by Respected Authors:

- If she enjoys reading, select books by respected authors or on topics related to her interests. Consider classic literature, business-related reads, or thought-provoking non-fiction.

9. Subscription to Professional Development Services:

- Support her professional growth by gifting a subscription to a professional development service, online courses, or a membership to a business-focused platform.

10. A Thoughtful Planner or Organizer: - Capricorn women often appreciate staying organized. Gift her a high-quality planner or organizer that aligns with her preferences, perhaps one with a sleek design and functional features.

11. A Timeless Fashion Piece: - Choose a timeless fashion piece, such as a tailored blazer, a classic coat, or a versatile pair of shoes. Opt for items that complement her style and withstand changing trends.

12. A Spa or Wellness Experience: - Treat her to a spa day or wellness experience. Consider a massage, facial, or a weekend getaway to a relaxing destination. This allows her to unwind and indulge in self-care.

13. Tickets to a Cultural or Professional Event: - Purchase tickets to a cultural event, art exhibition, or a professional conference related to her interests. This combines her appreciation for culture with opportunities for networking and learning.

14. Quality Kitchenware or Cookware: - If she enjoys cooking, consider gifting high-quality kitchenware or cookware. This could include a premium set of knives, stylish cookware, or unique culinary gadgets.

15. A Symbolic Gift Related to Her Goals: - Choose a gift that symbolizes her goals and aspirations. This could be a piece of artwork, a motivational book, or a custom-made item that reflects her journey.

Remember to consider her personal tastes and preferences when selecting a gift. Thoughtfulness and attention to detail go a long way in showing her that you appreciate her unique qualities as a Capricorn woman.

Capricorn History

The history of Capricorn, in the context of astrology, is rooted in ancient civilizations and the development of astrological systems. Astrology itself has a long history that spans cultures and civilizations, and the zodiac signs, including Capricorn, have evolved over centuries.

Here is a brief overview of the historical development of Capricorn in astrology:

1. **Ancient Mesopotamia:**

- The origins of astrology can be traced back to ancient Mesopotamia, particularly the Sumerians who developed early forms of celestial observation. The Babylonians later refined these observations, creating one of the earliest known astrological systems.

2. **Zodiac in Babylonia:**

- The zodiac, including the twelve signs, was established in Babylonia around the 5th century BCE. The Babylonians divided the ecliptic into twelve equal parts, each associated with a specific constellation. Capricorn was part of this zodiac system.

3. **Hellenistic Astrology:**

- Hellenistic astrology, influenced by Greek and Egyptian traditions, further developed the zodiac. The concept of the zodiac was adopted and adapted by various cultures in the Hellenistic world, including the Greeks and the Egyptians.

4. **Ptolemaic System:**

- The Hellenistic astrologer Claudius Ptolemy, in the 2nd century CE, played a significant role in shaping Western astrology. His work "Tetrabiblos" outlined the Ptolemaic system, which became the foundation for Western astrological practices. Capricorn is one of the zodiac signs in this system.

5. **Symbolism of Capricorn:**

- The symbol of Capricorn, often depicted as a sea-goat, has ancient roots. It is associated with the Sumerian god Enki, who was often depicted as a goat and had connections to water. The symbol represents the fusion of the earthy and ambitious qualities of the goat with the watery and intuitive nature of the fish.

6. Influence of Mythology:

- The symbolism of Capricorn is also influenced by mythology, particularly the myth of Pan in Greek mythology. Pan, a goat-legged deity, is associated with nature, wilderness, and the pursuit of goals. This imagery aligns with the determined and ambitious qualities associated with Capricorn.

7. Astrological Characteristics:

- Capricorn is an earth sign, ruled by the planet Saturn. It is often associated with qualities such as ambition, discipline, practicality, and a strong sense of responsibility. Capricorns are believed to be hardworking individuals who strive for success and stability.

8. Evolution in Modern Astrology:

- Modern astrology continues to incorporate and adapt the historical foundations of astrological knowledge. Capricorn, along with the other zodiac signs, is a key component of astrological charts and horoscopes used for personal insights and guidance.

It's important to note that astrology is a belief system that has been interpreted and practiced in various ways throughout history. While some people find value and meaning in astrological principles, others approach it with skepticism. The historical development of Capricorn is intertwined with the broader history of astrology and the cultural contexts in which it evolved.

The Myth Of Capricorn

The myth of Capricorn is often associated with the ancient Greek myth of Pan, a deity with a half-goat and half-fish appearance. While Pan is not directly linked to the zodiac sign of Capricorn, the imagery and symbolism of Pan have influenced the representation of Capricorn in astrology.

Here is a brief overview of the myth of Capricorn and its connection to Pan:

1. Pan in Greek Mythology:

- Pan is a rustic god in Greek mythology, often depicted as a creature with the lower body of a goat and the upper body of a human. He is associated with nature, shepherds, and the wild, representing the untamed aspects of the natural world.

2. The Birth of Pan:

- The most well-known myth associated with Pan's birth involves the nymph Syrinx. Pan pursued Syrinx, but she fled and prayed to the river god for help. In response, she was transformed into a clump of reeds. Pan, in his disappointment, crafted the first set of panpipes (a musical instrument) from the reeds, thus giving rise to the pan flute.

3. **Pan and the Sea-Goat Imagery:**

- While Pan is not directly linked to the zodiac sign of Capricorn in Greek mythology, the imagery of a creature with the lower body of a goat and the upper body of a human likely influenced the symbolism of Capricorn in astrology.

4. **Astrological Symbolism:**

- In astrology, Capricorn is often represented by a sea-goat, blending the characteristics of a goat with the tail of a fish. This symbolizes the earthly and ambitious qualities of the goat with the intuitive and emotional nature associated with the fish.

5. **The Sea-Goat Symbol in Capricorn:**

- The sea-goat symbolizes the ability of Capricorns to navigate both practical, earthly matters (represented by the goat) and emotional, intuitive realms (represented by the fish). It reflects the dual nature of Capricorn individuals, who are often characterized by their determination and sensitivity.

While the direct connection between Pan and Capricorn is not explicitly mentioned in ancient texts, the imagery and symbolism associated with Pan's goat-like appearance have influenced the representation of Capricorn in astrological traditions. The sea-goat symbolism captures the essence of Capricorn's qualities, blending the grounded and ambitious with the emotional and intuitive.

The connection between the Capricorn myth, particularly the influence of Pan, and the Capricorn zodiac sign is intriguing and symbolic. The derivation of the word "panic" from the name of the god Pan adds an interesting layer to the understanding of Capricorn's mythological roots.

The myth of Pan and its connection to the sign of Capricorn carries themes of fear, transformation, and the power of intimidation. The association of Pan with panic, stemming from the sound of the panikos instrument, further emphasizes the idea of fear scattering or dispersing like the Titans in the presence of this sound.

The symbolism of fear is significant in understanding the traits associated with Capricorn individuals. The zodiac sign of Capricorn is often characterized by a strong sense of responsibility, discipline, and a determined pursuit of goals. However, the myth suggests that fear plays a role in shaping the behavior and transformations associated with Capricorn.

The woman running away from compliments and the fear of a strange appearance in a dark place reflect the dual nature of Capricorn's symbolism—the goat and the fish. The goat represents the earthly, ambitious, and determined qualities, while the fish symbolizes the intuitive and emotional aspects. The fear depicted in the myth may symbolize the challenges and obstacles that Capricorn individuals face in their journey toward success and stability.

The transformation of Pan into a monster to scare away Typhon adds another layer to the theme of fear as a defensive mechanism. It highlights the idea that, in the face of challenges, Capricorn individuals may adopt different strategies, even transforming aspects of themselves to overcome obstacles and protect what they have built.

The lingering fear even after the battle is over speaks to the enduring nature of challenges and the constant need for vigilance. This mirrors the Capricorn trait of being cautious and vigilant in their endeavors, never fully letting their guard down.

The problems with the lower half of one's body in the myth may symbolize the vulnerabilities and challenges associated with the earthly or material aspects of life. Capricorns, while grounded and practical, may also grapple with issues related to their physical well-being or material concerns.

In summary, the connection between the Capricorn myth and the zodiac sign reflects themes of fear, transformation, and the enduring nature of challenges. It adds depth to the understanding of Capricorn's characteristics and the symbolic interplay between the goat and the fish in the astrological representation of this sign.

Capricorn Compatibility

Capricorn and Aries Compatibility:

In the cosmic dance of the zodiac, Capricorn and Aries set forth on a celestial journey, navigating the energies that define their unique connection. This exploration delves into the compatibility between the pragmatic Goat and the dynamic Ram.

Capricorn and Aries Compatibility Overview: Decoding the Celestial Alchemy of Earth and Fire

Let the compatibility percentage serve as our guiding star, shedding light on the intricate dynamics of the Capricorn and Aries union.

Compatibility Percentage: 70%

Capricorn in Love: Building Foundations in the Aries Inferno

Within the realm of love, the grounded nature of Capricorn encounters the fiery passion of Aries. This section unravels the sturdy and fervent dimensions of their cosmic connection.

Key Compatibility Traits: Unveiling Shared Bonds and Potential Challenges

Explore the foundational traits shaping the compatibility between Capricorn and Aries, uncovering the harmonious aspects and potential challenges in their cosmic union.

Stability and Spontaneity: Earth's Solid Ground Meets Fire's Unbridled Flame

The solid ground of Capricorn meets the unbridled flame of Aries. Discover how these distinct yet complementary energies intermingle, influencing the ebb and flow of their cosmic relationship.

Approaches to Risk and Caution: Bridging Capricorn's Prudence and Aries' Daring Ventures

In the dance of risk and caution, Capricorn's prudence meets Aries' daring ventures. Delve into how they navigate this delicate balance, forging a path that combines careful planning with spontaneous action.

Goal-Oriented Unity: Harmony in Aspirations and Shared Objectives

As goal-oriented souls unite, the alignment of aspirations and shared objectives becomes pivotal. Explore how Capricorn and Aries collaborate in achieving their individual and collective goals.

Challenges to Navigate: Addressing Potential Hurdles in the Capricorn-Aries Union

Beyond shared objectives, challenges may emerge. This section identifies potential stumbling blocks, offering insights into how Capricorn and Aries can navigate differences and foster understanding.

Capricorn-Aries Intimacy: Merging Earthly Foundations with Fiery Passions

In the intimate realms, the fusion of Capricorn's earthly foundations with Aries' fiery passions creates a unique blend. Understand how their intimate dynamics unfold, revealing the depth and richness of their cosmic connection.

Capricorn-Aries Friendship: Exploring Companionship Beyond Romance

Friendship is the cornerstone of enduring connections. Analyze how Capricorn and Aries navigate the realms of camaraderie, mutual support, and shared interests, adding another layer to their cosmic relationship.

Long-Term Outlook: Contemplating the Horizon of a Lasting Cosmic Bond

Peer into the cosmic horizon as we ponder the long-term prospects of Capricorn and Aries. Factors influencing the durability of their bond are scrutinized, providing a holistic view of their celestial journey.

Conclusion: Harmonizing Earth and Fire in the Capricorn-Aries Cosmic Symphony

In this cosmic exploration, traverse the diverse landscapes of Capricorn and Aries compatibility. The interplay of earth and fire energies creates a dynamic and evolving cosmic symphony, where stability meets spontaneity in the celestial dance of the Goat and the Ram.

Capricorn & Taurus

Capricorn and Taurus Compatibility:

In the cosmic dance of the zodiac, Capricorn and Taurus gracefully step into the celestial dance, intertwining their energies to create a harmonious connection. This exploration delves into the compatibility between the steadfast Goat and the grounded Bull.

Capricorn and Taurus Compatibility Overview: Decoding the Celestial Alchemy of Earth and Earth

Let the compatibility percentage illuminate the nuanced dynamics of the Capricorn and Taurus union.

Compatibility Percentage: 85%

Capricorn in Love: Building Earthly Foundations in the Taurus Embrace

Within the realm of love, the pragmatic heart of Capricorn encounters the nurturing embrace of Taurus. Unveil the robust and enduring dimensions of their cosmic connection.

Key Compatibility Traits: Unveiling Shared Bonds and Potential Challenges

Explore the foundational traits shaping the compatibility between Capricorn and Taurus, uncovering the harmonious aspects and potential challenges in their cosmic union.

Stability and Security: Earth's Solid Ground Finds Harmony in Taurus' Stable Embrace

The solid ground of Capricorn finds profound stability and security in the nurturing embrace of Taurus. Discover how these energies intermingle, influencing the ebb and flow of their cosmic relationship.

Material Goals and Practical Pursuits: Aligning Ambitions and Ensuring Practical Success

As two earth signs unite, their alignment in material goals and practical pursuits becomes a cornerstone of their compatibility. Explore how Capricorn and Taurus collaborate in achieving tangible success.

Approaches to Finance and Resources: Bridging Capricorn's Financial Prudence with Taurus' Resourcefulness

In the realm of finances and resources, Capricorn's financial prudence meets Taurus' resourcefulness. Delve into how they navigate financial matters, forging a path that combines careful planning with resourceful strategies.

Home and Family Life: Creating a Solid Domestic Foundation

The shared desire for a stable home and family life forms a solid foundation for Capricorn and Taurus. Explore how they navigate the realms of domesticity, mutual support, and shared responsibilities.

Challenges to Navigate: Addressing Potential Hurdles in the Capricorn-Taurus Union

Despite shared goals, challenges may arise. This section identifies potential stumbling blocks, offering insights into how Capricorn and Taurus can navigate differences and foster understanding.

Capricorn-Taurus Intimacy: Merging Earthly Passions with Sensual Depths

In the intimate realms, the fusion of Capricorn's earthly passions with Taurus' sensual depths creates a unique blend. Understand how their intimate dynamics unfold, revealing the depth and richness of their cosmic connection.

Capricorn-Taurus Friendship: Exploring Companionship Beyond Romance

Friendship is the cornerstone of enduring connections. Analyze how Capricorn and Taurus navigate the realms of camaraderie, mutual support, and shared interests, adding another layer to their cosmic relationship.

Long-Term Outlook: Contemplating the Horizon of a Lasting Cosmic Bond

Peer into the cosmic horizon as we ponder the long-term prospects of Capricorn and Taurus. Factors influencing the durability of their bond are scrutinized, providing a holistic view of their celestial journey.

Conclusion: Harmonizing Earth Energies in the Capricorn-Taurus Cosmic Symphony

In this cosmic exploration, traverse the diverse landscapes of Capricorn and Taurus compatibility. The interplay of earth energies creates a dynamic and enduring cosmic symphony, where stability meets sensuality in the celestial dance of the Goat and the Bull.

Capricorn & Gemini

Capricorn and Gemini Compatibility:

In the cosmic ballet of the zodiac, Capricorn and Gemini step into the celestial dance, blending their energies in a unique cosmic symphony. This exploration delves into the compatibility between the pragmatic Goat and the versatile Twins.

Capricorn and Gemini Compatibility Overview: Decoding the Celestial Alchemy of Earth and Air

Let the compatibility percentage illuminate the nuanced dynamics of the Capricorn and Gemini union.

Compatibility Percentage: 60%

Capricorn in Love: Navigating the Airy Realms of Gemini's Affection

Within the realm of love, the grounded nature of Capricorn encounters the airy affection of Gemini. Unveil the sturdy and adaptable dimensions of their cosmic connection.

Key Compatibility Traits: Unveiling Shared Bonds and Potential Challenges

Explore the foundational traits shaping the compatibility between Capricorn and Gemini, uncovering the harmonious aspects and potential challenges in their cosmic union.

Practicality and Versatility: Earth's Practicality Meets Air's Versatile Winds

The practicality of Capricorn meets the versatile winds of Gemini. Discover how these distinct yet complementary energies intermingle, influencing the ebb and flow of their cosmic relationship.

Communication Styles: Bridging Earthly Expressions and Airy Insights

Communication, the celestial language, plays a pivotal role in this union. Delve into how Capricorn's grounded expressions align with Gemini's intellectual insights, shaping their ability to convey thoughts and feelings.

Approaches to Stability and Change: Harmony in Navigating Stability Amidst Gemini's Change

As stability-seeking Capricorn encounters Gemini's love for change, a delicate balance is struck. Explore how they navigate the dance between stability and change, finding common ground in their unique approaches.

Shared Goals and Personal Ambitions: Aligning Aspirations in the Cosmic Pursuit

Capricorn and Gemini align in their pursuit of goals and ambitions. Explore how their shared visions and personal aspirations create a foundation for mutual understanding.

Challenges to Navigate: Addressing Potential Hurdles in the Capricorn-Gemini Union

Beyond shared goals, challenges may emerge. This section identifies potential stumbling blocks, offering insights into how Capricorn and Gemini can navigate differences and foster understanding.

Capricorn-Gemini Intimacy: Merging Earthly Passions with Airy Affection

In the intimate realms, the fusion of Capricorn's earthly passions with Gemini's airy affection creates a unique blend. Understand how their intimate dynamics unfold, revealing the depth and richness of their cosmic connection.

Capricorn-Gemini Friendship: Exploring Companionship Beyond Romance

Friendship forms the bedrock of enduring connections. Analyze how Capricorn and Gemini navigate the realms of camaraderie, mutual support, and shared interests, adding another layer to their cosmic relationship.

Long-Term Outlook: Contemplating the Horizon of a Lasting Cosmic Bond

Peer into the cosmic horizon as we ponder the long-term prospects of Capricorn and Gemini. Factors influencing the durability of their bond are scrutinized, providing a holistic view of their celestial journey.

Conclusion: Balancing Earth and Air in the Capricorn-Gemini Cosmic Symphony

In this cosmic exploration, traverse the diverse landscapes of Capricorn and Gemini compatibility. The interplay of earth and air energies creates a dynamic and evolving cosmic symphony, where stability meets versatility in the celestial dance of the Goat and the Twins.

Capricorn & Cancer

Capricorn and Cancer Compatibility:

In the cosmic choreography of the zodiac, Capricorn and Cancer gracefully join the celestial dance, blending their energies in a unique cosmic symphony. This exploration delves into the compatibility between the pragmatic Goat and the nurturing Crab.

Capricorn and Cancer Compatibility Overview: Decoding the Celestial Alchemy of Earth and Water

Let the compatibility percentage illuminate the nuanced dynamics of the Capricorn and Cancer union.

Compatibility Percentage: 75%

Capricorn in Love: Building Foundations in Cancer's Protective Embrace

Within the realm of love, the grounded nature of Capricorn encounters the protective embrace of Cancer. Unveil the sturdy and emotionally rich dimensions of their cosmic connection.

Key Compatibility Traits: Unveiling Shared Bonds and Potential Challenges

Explore the foundational traits shaping the compatibility between Capricorn and Cancer, uncovering the harmonious aspects and potential challenges in their cosmic union.

Stability and Emotion: Earth's Solid Ground Meets the Depths of Cancer's Emotion

The solid ground of Capricorn finds resonance in the emotional depths of Cancer. Discover how these energies intermingle, influencing the ebb and flow of their cosmic relationship.

Approaches to Security and Comfort: Bridging Capricorn's Quest for Security with Cancer's Need for Comfort

In the dance of security and comfort, Capricorn's quest for stability meets Cancer's need for emotional comfort. Delve into how they navigate this delicate balance, creating a space where both feel secure and nurtured.

Family Values and Domestic Life: Harmony in Nurturing a Shared Home

Capricorn and Cancer align in their values of family and domestic life. Explore how their shared commitment to creating a nurturing home becomes the cornerstone of their compatibility.

Shared Goals and Personal Ambitions: Aligning Aspirations in the Cosmic Pursuit

Capricorn and Cancer find alignment in their pursuit of shared goals and personal ambitions. Explore how their collaborative visions create a foundation for mutual understanding and growth.

Challenges to Navigate: Addressing Potential Hurdles in the Capricorn-Cancer Union

Despite shared goals, challenges may emerge. This section identifies potential stumbling blocks, offering insights into how Capricorn and Cancer can navigate differences and foster understanding.

Capricorn-Cancer Intimacy: Merging Earthly Passions with Water's Emotional Depths

In the intimate realms, the fusion of Capricorn's earthly passions with Cancer's emotional depths creates a unique blend. Understand how their intimate dynamics unfold, revealing the depth and richness of their cosmic connection.

Capricorn-Cancer Friendship: Exploring Companionship Beyond Romance

Friendship forms the bedrock of enduring connections. Analyze how Capricorn and Cancer navigate the realms of camaraderie, mutual support, and shared interests, adding another layer to their cosmic relationship.

Long-Term Outlook: Contemplating the Horizon of a Lasting Cosmic Bond

Peer into the cosmic horizon as we ponder the long-term prospects of Capricorn and Cancer. Factors influencing the durability of their bond are scrutinized, providing a holistic view of their celestial journey.

Conclusion: Balancing Earth and Water in the Capricorn-Cancer Cosmic Symphony

In this cosmic exploration, traverse the diverse landscapes of Capricorn and Cancer compatibility. The interplay of earth and water energies creates a dynamic and evolving cosmic symphony, where stability meets emotional depth in the celestial dance of the Goat and the Crab.

Capricorn and Leo Compatibility:

In the grand celestial ballet, Capricorn and Leo take center stage, blending their energies in a unique cosmic dance. This exploration delves into the compatibility between the pragmatic Goat and the bold Lion.

Capricorn and Leo Compatibility Overview: Decoding the Celestial Alchemy of Earth and Fire

Let the compatibility percentage illuminate the nuanced dynamics of the Capricorn and Leo union.

Compatibility Percentage: 70%

Capricorn in Love: Finding Ground in the Leo's Fiery Affection

Within the realm of love, the grounded nature of Capricorn encounters the passionate affection of Leo. Unveil the sturdy and fiery dimensions of their cosmic connection.

Key Compatibility Traits: Unveiling Shared Bonds and Potential Challenges

Explore the foundational traits shaping the compatibility between Capricorn and Leo, uncovering the harmonious aspects and potential challenges in their cosmic union.

Stability and Passion: Earth's Solid Ground Meets the Fiery Passion of Leo

The solid ground of Capricorn finds resonance in the fiery passion of Leo. Discover how these energies intermingle, influencing the ebb and flow of their cosmic relationship.

Approaches to Leadership and Recognition: Bridging Capricorn's Practical Leadership with Leo's Need for Recognition

In the dance of leadership and recognition, Capricorn's practical approach meets Leo's desire for acknowledgment. Delve into how they navigate this delicate balance, finding a space where both can shine in their unique ways.

Ambitions and Creative Pursuits: Harmony in Aspiring to Reach Heights Together

Capricorn and Leo align in their ambitions and creative pursuits. Explore how their collaborative visions create a foundation for mutual growth and success.

Individual Independence and Shared Goals: Balancing Autonomy in the Pursuit of Common Objectives

As two independent souls unite, finding the balance between individual autonomy and shared goals becomes crucial. Explore how Capricorn and Leo navigate this intricate dance, forging a path of mutual understanding.

Challenges to Navigate: Addressing Potential Hurdles in the Capricorn-Leo Union

Despite shared goals, challenges may emerge. This section identifies potential stumbling blocks, offering insights into how Capricorn and Leo can navigate differences and foster understanding.

Capricorn-Leo Intimacy: Merging Earthly Passions with Leo's Fiery Depths

In the intimate realms, the fusion of Capricorn's earthly passions with Leo's fiery depths creates a unique blend. Understand how their intimate dynamics unfold, revealing the depth and richness of their cosmic connection.

Capricorn-Leo Friendship: Exploring Companionship Beyond Romance

Friendship forms the bedrock of enduring connections. Analyze how Capricorn and Leo navigate the realms of camaraderie, mutual support, and shared interests, adding another layer to their cosmic relationship.

Long-Term Outlook: Contemplating the Horizon of a Lasting Cosmic Bond

Peer into the cosmic horizon as we ponder the long-term prospects of Capricorn and Leo. Factors influencing the durability of their bond are scrutinized, providing a holistic view of their celestial journey.

Conclusion: Balancing Earth and Fire in the Capricorn-Leo Cosmic Symphony

In this cosmic exploration, traverse the diverse landscapes of Capricorn and Leo compatibility. The interplay of earth and fire energies creates a dynamic and evolving cosmic symphony, where stability meets passion in the celestial dance of the Goat and the Lion.

Capricorn and Virgo Compatibility:

In the celestial choreography of the zodiac, Capricorn and Virgo take the stage, intertwining their energies in a unique cosmic dance. This exploration delves into the compatibility between the pragmatic Goat and the analytical Virgin.

Capricorn and Virgo Compatibility Overview: Decoding the Celestial Alchemy of Earth and Earth

Let the compatibility percentage illuminate the nuanced dynamics of the Capricorn and Virgo union.

Compatibility Percentage: 80%

Capricorn in Love: Building Foundations in Virgo's Meticulous Affection

Within the realm of love, the grounded nature of Capricorn encounters the meticulous affection of Virgo. Unveil the sturdy and detail-oriented dimensions of their cosmic connection.

Key Compatibility Traits: Unveiling Shared Bonds and Potential Challenges

Explore the foundational traits shaping the compatibility between Capricorn and Virgo, uncovering the harmonious aspects and potential challenges in their cosmic union.

Stability and Practicality: Earth's Solid Ground Meets Virgo's Pragmatic Approach

The solid ground of Capricorn finds resonance in Virgo's practicality. Discover how these energies intermingle, influencing the ebb and flow of their cosmic relationship.

Approaches to Work and Responsibilities: Bridging Capricorn's Work Ethic with Virgo's Attention to Detail

In the dance of work and responsibilities, Capricorn's strong work ethic meets Virgo's meticulous attention to detail. Delve into how they navigate this delicate balance, creating a productive and organized partnership.

Shared Values and Material Goals: Harmony in Aligning Material Aspirations

Capricorn and Virgo align seamlessly in their values and material goals. Explore how their shared aspirations create a solid foundation for mutual growth and achievement.

Communication Styles: Balancing Earthly Expressions for Effective Communication

Communication, the celestial language, plays a pivotal role in this union. Explore how Capricorn's grounded expressions align with Virgo's analytical communication style, fostering effective understanding.

Challenges to Navigate: Addressing Potential Hurdles in the Capricorn-Virgo Union

Despite shared values, challenges may emerge. This section identifies potential stumbling blocks, offering insights into how Capricorn and Virgo can navigate differences and foster understanding.

Capricorn-Virgo Intimacy: Merging Earthly Passions with Virgo's Thoughtful Depths

In the intimate realms, the fusion of Capricorn's earthly passions with Virgo's thoughtful depths creates a unique blend. Understand how their intimate dynamics unfold, revealing the depth and richness of their cosmic connection.

Capricorn-Virgo Friendship: Exploring Companionship Beyond Romance

Friendship forms the bedrock of enduring connections. Analyze how Capricorn and Virgo navigate the realms of camaraderie, mutual support, and shared interests, adding another layer to their cosmic relationship.

Long-Term Outlook: Contemplating the Horizon of a Lasting Cosmic Bond

Peer into the cosmic horizon as we ponder the long-term prospects of Capricorn and Virgo. Factors influencing the durability of their bond are scrutinized, providing a holistic view of their celestial journey.

Conclusion: Balancing Earth in the Capricorn-Virgo Cosmic Symphony

In this cosmic exploration, traverse the diverse landscapes of Capricorn and Virgo compatibility. The interplay of earth energies creates a dynamic and evolving cosmic symphony, where stability meets practicality in the celestial dance of the Goat and the Virgin.

Capricorn and Libra Compatibility:

In the cosmic ballet of the zodiac, Capricorn and Libra gracefully dance together, blending their energies in a unique cosmic symphony. This exploration delves into the compatibility between the pragmatic Goat and the harmonious Scales.

Capricorn and Libra Compatibility Overview: Decoding the Celestial Alchemy of Earth and Air

Let the compatibility percentage serve as our guiding star, shedding light on the intricate dynamics of the Capricorn and Libra union.

Compatibility Percentage: 65%

Capricorn in Love: Building Foundations in Libra's Balancing Affection

Within the realm of love, the grounded nature of Capricorn encounters the balancing affection of Libra. Unveil the sturdy and harmonious dimensions of their cosmic connection.

Key Compatibility Traits: Unveiling Shared Bonds and Potential Challenges

Explore the foundational traits shaping the compatibility between Capricorn and Libra, uncovering the harmonious aspects and potential challenges in their cosmic union.

Stability and Harmony: Earth's Solid Ground Meets Libra's Quest for Balance

The solid ground of Capricorn finds resonance in Libra's quest for harmony. Discover how these energies intermingle, influencing the ebb and flow of their cosmic relationship.

Approaches to Decision-Making and Diplomacy: Bridging Capricorn's Practical Decisions with Libra's Diplomatic Style

In the dance of decision-making and diplomacy, Capricorn's practical approach meets Libra's diplomatic style. Delve into how they navigate this delicate balance, creating a blend of pragmatism and diplomacy.

Values and Relationship Ideals: Harmony in Aligning Values for Relationship Success

Capricorn and Libra align in their values and relationship ideals. Explore how their shared aspirations create a foundation for mutual understanding and growth.

Communication Styles: Balancing Earthly Realism with Airy Expressiveness

Communication, the celestial language, plays a pivotal role in this union. Explore how Capricorn's grounded realism aligns with Libra's expressive communication style, fostering effective understanding.

Challenges to Navigate: Addressing Potential Hurdles in the Capricorn-Libra Union

Despite shared values, challenges may emerge. This section identifies potential stumbling blocks, offering insights into how Capricorn and Libra can navigate differences and foster understanding.

Capricorn-Libra Intimacy: Merging Earthly Passions with Libra's Romantic Depths

In the intimate realms, the fusion of Capricorn's earthly passions with Libra's romantic depths creates a unique blend.

Understand how their intimate dynamics unfold, revealing the depth and richness of their cosmic connection.

Capricorn-Libra Friendship: Exploring Companionship Beyond Romance

Friendship forms the bedrock of enduring connections. Analyze how Capricorn and Libra navigate the realms of camaraderie, mutual support, and shared interests, adding another layer to their cosmic relationship.

Long-Term Outlook: Contemplating the Horizon of a Lasting Cosmic Bond

Peer into the cosmic horizon as we ponder the long-term prospects of Capricorn and Libra. Factors influencing the durability of their bond are scrutinized, providing a holistic view of their celestial journey.

Conclusion: Balancing Earth and Air in the Capricorn-Libra Cosmic Symphony

In this cosmic exploration, traverse the diverse landscapes of Capricorn and Libra compatibility. The interplay of earth and air energies creates a dynamic and evolving cosmic symphony, where stability meets harmony in the celestial dance of the Goat and the Scales.

Capricorn and Scorpio Compatibility:

In the cosmic ballet of the zodiac, Capricorn and Scorpio join hands, engaging in a passionate and intense dance that weaves their energies into a unique cosmic tapestry. This exploration delves into the compatibility between the pragmatic Goat and the mysterious Scorpion.

Capricorn and Scorpio Compatibility Overview: Decoding the Celestial Alchemy of Earth and Water

Let the compatibility percentage serve as our guiding star, shedding light on the intricate dynamics of the Capricorn and Scorpio union.

Compatibility Percentage: 85%

Capricorn in Love: Building Foundations in Scorpio's Deep Waters

Within the realm of love, the grounded nature of Capricorn encounters the deep waters of Scorpio. Unveil the sturdy and intense dimensions of their cosmic connection.

Key Compatibility Traits: Unveiling Shared Bonds and Potential Challenges

Explore the foundational traits shaping the compatibility between Capricorn and Scorpio, uncovering the harmonious aspects and potential challenges in their cosmic union.

Stability and Emotional Depth: Earth's Solid Ground Meets Scorpio's Profound Emotions

The solid ground of Capricorn finds resonance in Scorpio's profound emotional depths. Discover how these energies intermingle, influencing the ebb and flow of their cosmic relationship.

Approaches to Trust and Loyalty: Bridging Capricorn's Trustworthiness with Scorpio's Loyalty

In the dance of trust and loyalty, Capricorn's trustworthiness meets Scorpio's unwavering loyalty. Delve into how they navigate this delicate balance, creating a foundation of mutual trust and commitment.

Shared Goals and Transformative Ambitions: Harmony in Aligning Ambitions for Mutual Growth

Capricorn and Scorpio align seamlessly in their goals and transformative ambitions. Explore how their shared aspirations create a solid foundation for mutual growth and evolution.

Communication Styles: Balancing Earthly Realism with Watery Intuition

Communication, the celestial language, plays a pivotal role in this union. Explore how Capricorn's grounded realism aligns with Scorpio's intuitive communication style, fostering a deep understanding.

Challenges to Navigate: Addressing Potential Hurdles in the Capricorn-Scorpio Union

Despite shared goals, challenges may emerge. This section identifies potential stumbling blocks, offering insights into how Capricorn and Scorpio can navigate differences and foster understanding.

Capricorn-Scorpio Intimacy: Merging Earthly Passion with Scorpio's Profound Connection

In the intimate realms, the fusion of Capricorn's earthly passion with Scorpio's profound connection creates a unique blend. Understand how their intimate dynamics unfold, revealing the depth and richness of their cosmic connection.

Capricorn-Scorpio Friendship: Exploring Companionship Beyond Romance

Friendship forms the bedrock of enduring connections. Analyze how Capricorn and Scorpio navigate the realms of camaraderie, mutual support, and shared interests, adding another layer to their cosmic relationship.

Long-Term Outlook: Contemplating the Horizon of a Lasting Cosmic Bond

Peer into the cosmic horizon as we ponder the long-term prospects of Capricorn and Scorpio. Factors influencing the durability of their bond are scrutinized, providing a holistic view of their celestial journey.

Conclusion: Harmonizing Earth and Water in the Capricorn-Scorpio Cosmic Symphony

In this cosmic exploration, traverse the diverse landscapes of Capricorn and Scorpio compatibility. The interplay of earth and water energies creates a dynamic and evolving cosmic symphony, where stability meets emotional depth in the celestial dance of the Goat and the Scorpion.

Capricorn and Sagittarius Compatibility:

In the cosmic waltz of the zodiac, Capricorn and Sagittarius come together, twirling in a dance that blends their energies into a unique cosmic harmony. This exploration delves into the compatibility between the pragmatic Goat and the adventurous Archer.

Capricorn and Sagittarius Compatibility Overview: Decoding the Celestial Alchemy of Earth and Fire

Let the compatibility percentage serve as our guiding star, shedding light on the intricate dynamics of the Capricorn and Sagittarius union.

Compatibility Percentage: 75%

Capricorn in Love: Building Foundations in Sagittarius' Fiery Passion

Within the realm of love, the grounded nature of Capricorn encounters the fiery passion of Sagittarius. Unveil the sturdy and adventurous dimensions of their cosmic connection.

Key Compatibility Traits: Unveiling Shared Bonds and Potential Challenges

Explore the foundational traits shaping the compatibility between Capricorn and Sagittarius, uncovering the harmonious aspects and potential challenges in their cosmic union.

Stability and Adventurous Spirit: Earth's Solid Ground Meets Sagittarius' Quest for Exploration

The solid ground of Capricorn finds resonance in Sagittarius' adventurous spirit. Discover how these energies intermingle, influencing the ebb and flow of their cosmic relationship.

Approaches to Planning and Spontaneity: Bridging Capricorn's Strategic Planning with Sagittarius' Spontaneous Nature

In the dance of planning and spontaneity, Capricorn's strategic planning meets Sagittarius' spontaneous nature. Delve into how they navigate this delicate balance, creating a blend of stability and excitement.

Shared Values and Philosophies: Harmony in Aligning Values for a Fulfilling Journey

Capricorn and Sagittarius align seamlessly in their values and life philosophies. Explore how their shared aspirations create a foundation for mutual understanding and a fulfilling journey.

Communication Styles: Balancing Earthly Realism with Fiery Enthusiasm

Communication, the celestial language, plays a pivotal role in this union. Explore how Capricorn's grounded realism aligns with Sagittarius' enthusiastic communication style, fostering effective understanding.

Challenges to Navigate: Addressing Potential Hurdles in the Capricorn-Sagittarius Union

Despite shared values, challenges may emerge. This section identifies potential stumbling blocks, offering insights into how Capricorn and Sagittarius can navigate differences and foster understanding.

Capricorn-Sagittarius Intimacy: Merging Earthly Passion with Sagittarius' Spontaneous Romance

In the intimate realms, the fusion of Capricorn's earthly passion with Sagittarius' spontaneous romance creates a unique blend. Understand how their intimate dynamics unfold, revealing the depth and richness of their cosmic connection.

Capricorn-Sagittarius Friendship: Exploring Companionship Beyond Romance

Friendship forms the bedrock of enduring connections. Analyze how Capricorn and Sagittarius navigate the realms of camaraderie, mutual support, and shared interests, adding another layer to their cosmic relationship.

Long-Term Outlook: Contemplating the Horizon of a Lasting Cosmic Bond

Peer into the cosmic horizon as we ponder the long-term prospects of Capricorn and Sagittarius. Factors influencing the durability of their bond are scrutinized, providing a holistic view of their celestial journey.

Conclusion: Harmonizing Earth and Fire in the Capricorn-Sagittarius Cosmic Symphony

In this cosmic exploration, traverse the diverse landscapes of Capricorn and Sagittarius compatibility. The interplay of earth and fire energies creates a dynamic and evolving cosmic symphony, where stability meets adventure in the celestial dance of the Goat and the Archer.

Capricorn and Capricorn Compatibility:

In the celestial duet of the zodiac, two Capricorns unite, creating a harmonious yet pragmatic cosmic melody. This exploration delves into the compatibility between two pragmatic Goats, examining how their shared traits and nuances shape their cosmic connection.

Capricorn and Capricorn Compatibility Overview: Decoding the Celestial Alchemy of Earth and Earth

Let the compatibility percentage serve as our guiding star, shedding light on the intricate dynamics of the Capricorn and Capricorn union.

Compatibility Percentage: 90%

Capricorn in Love: Building Foundations in Tandem Earthly Commitment

Within the realm of love, the grounded nature of Capricorn encounters its mirror image in another Capricorn. Unveil the sturdy and committed dimensions of their cosmic connection.

Key Compatibility Traits: Unveiling Shared Bonds and Potential Challenges

Explore the foundational traits shaping the compatibility between two Capricorns, uncovering the harmonious aspects and potential challenges in their cosmic union.

Stability and Practicality: Tandem Earth's Solid Ground and Shared Practicality

The solid ground of Capricorn meets its reflection in another Capricorn, creating a foundation of stability and shared practicality. Discover how these energies intermingle, influencing the ebb and flow of their cosmic relationship.

Approaches to Goals and Achievements: Twin Goats Climbing the Summit of Ambitions

In the pursuit of goals and achievements, two Capricorns climb together toward the summit. Delve into how their shared ambitions create a pathway for mutual success and accomplishment.

Shared Values and Life Philosophies: Harmony in Echoing Values for a Purposeful Journey

Two Capricorns echo each other in values and life philosophies. Explore how their shared aspirations create a foundation for mutual understanding and a purposeful journey.

Communication Styles: Balancing Earthly Realism with Pragmatic Expression

Communication, the celestial language, plays a pivotal role in this union. Explore how two Capricorns' grounded realism aligns, fostering effective understanding and pragmatic expression.

Challenges to Navigate: Addressing Potential Hurdles in the Capricorn-Capricorn Union

Despite shared values, challenges may emerge. This section identifies potential stumbling blocks, offering insights into how two Capricorns can navigate differences and foster understanding.

Capricorn-Capricorn Intimacy: Merging Earthly Passions with Tandem Devotion

In the intimate realms, the fusion of Capricorn's earthly passions finds a mirror in the devotion of another Capricorn, creating a unique blend. Understand how their intimate dynamics unfold, revealing the depth and richness of their cosmic connection.

Capricorn-Capricorn Friendship: Exploring Companionship Beyond Romance

Friendship forms the bedrock of enduring connections. Analyze how two Capricorns navigate the realms of camaraderie, mutual support, and shared interests, adding another layer to their cosmic relationship.

Long-Term Outlook: Contemplating the Horizon of a Lasting Cosmic Bond

Peer into the cosmic horizon as we ponder the long-term prospects of two Capricorns. Factors influencing the durability of their bond are scrutinized, providing a holistic view of their celestial journey.

Conclusion: Harmonizing Earth with Earth in the Capricorn-Capricorn Cosmic Symphony

In this cosmic exploration, traverse the diverse landscapes of Capricorn and Capricorn compatibility. The symphony of two earth energies creates a dynamic and enduring cosmic melody, where stability meets commitment in the celestial dance of the dual Goats.

Capricorn and Aquarius Compatibility:

In the cosmic alliance of the zodiac, Capricorn and Aquarius join forces, blending their energies in a unique cosmic dance. This exploration delves into the compatibility between the pragmatic Goat and the visionary Water Bearer.

Capricorn and Aquarius Compatibility Overview: Decoding the Celestial Alchemy of Earth and Air

Let the compatibility percentage serve as our guiding star, shedding light on the intricate dynamics of the Capricorn and Aquarius union.

Compatibility Percentage: 80%

Capricorn in Love: Building Foundations in Aquarius' Intellectual Waters

Within the realm of love, the grounded nature of Capricorn encounters the intellectual waters of Aquarius. Unveil the sturdy and visionary dimensions of their cosmic connection.

Key Compatibility Traits: Unveiling Shared Bonds and Potential Challenges

Explore the foundational traits shaping the compatibility between Capricorn and Aquarius, uncovering the harmonious aspects and potential challenges in their cosmic union.

Stability and Innovation: Earth's Solid Ground Meets Air's Unconventional Ideas

The solid ground of Capricorn finds resonance in Aquarius' innovative ideas, creating a blend of stability and creativity. Discover how these energies intermingle, influencing the ebb and flow of their cosmic relationship.

Approaches to Tradition and Progress: Bridging Capricorn's Traditionalism with Aquarius' Progressive Spirit

In the dance of tradition and progress, Capricorn's traditionalism meets Aquarius' progressive spirit. Delve into how they navigate this delicate balance, forging a path that combines respect for tradition with openness to new ideas.

Shared Values and Humanitarian Goals: Harmony in Aligning Values for a Purposeful Journey

Capricorn and Aquarius align seamlessly in their values and humanitarian goals. Explore how their shared aspirations create a foundation for mutual understanding and a purposeful journey.

Communication Styles: Balancing Earthly Realism with Airy Idealism

Communication, the celestial language, plays a pivotal role in this union. Explore how Capricorn's grounded realism aligns with Aquarius' airy idealism, fostering effective understanding and innovative expression.

Challenges to Navigate: Addressing Potential Hurdles in the Capricorn-Aquarius Union

Despite shared values, challenges may emerge. This section identifies potential stumbling blocks, offering insights into how Capricorn and Aquarius can navigate differences and foster understanding.

Capricorn-Aquarius Intimacy: Merging Earthly Passion with Aquarius' Intellectual Depth

In the intimate realms, the fusion of Capricorn's earthly passion meets Aquarius' intellectual depth, creating a unique blend. Understand how their intimate dynamics unfold, revealing the depth and richness of their cosmic connection.

Capricorn-Aquarius Friendship: Exploring Companionship Beyond Romance

Friendship forms the bedrock of enduring connections. Analyze how Capricorn and Aquarius navigate the realms of camaraderie, mutual support, and shared interests, adding another layer to their cosmic relationship.

Long-Term Outlook: Contemplating the Horizon of a Lasting Cosmic Bond

Peer into the cosmic horizon as we ponder the long-term prospects of Capricorn and Aquarius. Factors influencing the durability of their bond are scrutinized, providing a holistic view of their celestial journey.

Conclusion: Harmonizing Earth and Air in the Capricorn-Aquarius Cosmic Symphony

In this cosmic exploration, traverse the diverse landscapes of Capricorn and Aquarius compatibility. The interplay of earth and air energies creates a dynamic and evolving cosmic symphony, where stability meets innovation in the celestial dance of the Goat and the Water Bearer.

Capricorn and Pisces Compatibility:

In the cosmic ballet of the zodiac, Capricorn and Pisces join hands, dancing to the rhythm of their unique energies. This exploration delves into the compatibility between the pragmatic Goat and the dreamy Fish.

Capricorn and Pisces Compatibility Overview: Decoding the Celestial Alchemy of Earth and Water

Let the compatibility percentage serve as our guiding star, shedding light on the intricate dynamics of the Capricorn and Pisces union.

Compatibility Percentage: 85%

Capricorn in Love: Building Foundations in Pisces' Emotional Depths

Within the realm of love, the grounded nature of Capricorn encounters the emotional depths of Pisces. Unveil the sturdy and empathetic dimensions of their cosmic connection.

Key Compatibility Traits: Unveiling Shared Bonds and Potential Challenges

Explore the foundational traits shaping the compatibility between Capricorn and Pisces, uncovering the harmonious aspects and potential challenges in their cosmic union.

Stability and Sensitivity: Earth's Solid Ground Meets Water's Emotional Currents

The solid ground of Capricorn finds resonance in Pisces' emotional currents, creating a blend of stability and sensitivity. Discover how these energies intermingle, influencing the ebb and flow of their cosmic relationship.

Practicality and Imagination: Bridging Capricorn's Practicality with Pisces' Creative Imagination

In the dance of practicality and imagination, Capricorn's practical nature meets Pisces' creative imagination. Delve into how they navigate this delicate balance, forging a path that combines realism with dreamy creativity.

Shared Values and Compassionate Goals: Harmony in Aligning Values for a Purposeful Journey

Capricorn and Pisces align seamlessly in their values and compassionate goals. Explore how their shared aspirations create a foundation for mutual understanding and a purposeful journey.

Communication Styles: Balancing Earthly Realism with Watery Intuition

Communication, the celestial language, plays a pivotal role in this union. Explore how Capricorn's grounded realism aligns with Pisces' intuitive communication style, fostering effective understanding and emotional connection.

Challenges to Navigate: Addressing Potential Hurdles in the Capricorn-Pisces Union

Despite shared values, challenges may emerge. This section identifies potential stumbling blocks, offering insights into how Capricorn and Pisces can navigate differences and foster understanding.

Capricorn-Pisces Intimacy: Merging Earthly Passion with Pisces' Soulful Connection

In the intimate realms, the fusion of Capricorn's earthly passion meets Pisces' soulful connection, creating a unique blend. Understand how their intimate dynamics unfold, revealing the depth and richness of their cosmic connection.

Capricorn-Pisces Friendship: Exploring Companionship Beyond Romance

Friendship forms the bedrock of enduring connections. Analyze how Capricorn and Pisces navigate the realms of camaraderie, mutual support, and shared interests, adding another layer to their cosmic relationship.

Long-Term Outlook: Contemplating the Horizon of a Lasting Cosmic Bond

Peer into the cosmic horizon as we ponder the long-term prospects of Capricorn and Pisces. Factors influencing the durability of their bond are scrutinized, providing a holistic view of their celestial journey.

Conclusion: Harmonizing Earth and Water in the Capricorn-Pisces Cosmic Symphony

In this cosmic exploration, traverse the diverse landscapes of Capricorn and Pisces compatibility. The interplay of earth and water energies creates a dynamic and evolving cosmic symphony, where stability meets emotion in the celestial dance of the Goat and the Fish.

Frequently Asked Questions:

1. How will this year 2024 be for Capricorn individuals?

- Capricorn natives can expect a positive financial outlook in 2024, allowing them to settle old debts.

2. When will the fortune of Capricorns rise in 2024?

- Favorable outcomes for Capricorns are predicted to start manifesting from May 2024 onwards.

3. What is the destiny of Capricorn at the moment?

- Currently, destiny is in favor of Capricorns, offering them the fulfillment of their desires.

4. Who is considered the soulmate of Capricorn?

- Virgo is often believed to be the soulmate of Capricorn, with a harmonious connection between these two signs.

5. Which zodiac signs are compatible with and love Capricorn?

- Capricorn is said to be compatible with Virgo and Taurus, suggesting strong and positive connections.

6. Which zodiac signs are considered enemies of Capricorn?

- Aquarius, Leo, and Gemini are often considered less compatible with Capricorn, potentially leading to challenges in relationships.

Frequently Asked Questions About Capricorn Women:

1. What are the key personality traits of Capricorn women?

- Capricorn women are known for their traditional and serious nature. They exhibit a strong sense of independence, are skilled in self-control, and are capable of making realistic plans.

2. How do Capricorn women handle relationships?

- Capricorn women approach relationships with a sense of responsibility. They learn from their mistakes, rely on their experience, and are committed to making significant progress in their personal lives.

3. What is the ruling planet of Capricorn women and its influence?

- The ruling planet of Capricorn women is Saturn, representing restriction. While it makes them practical and responsible, it can also make them appear cold and distant. Forgiveness is crucial for Capricorn women to lighten their lives.

4. Can you trust a Capricorn woman?

- Capricorn women are generally trustworthy and reliable. They value commitment and stability in relationships, making them dependable partners.

5. What is the ideal match for a Capricorn woman?

- Virgo is often considered an ideal match for Capricorn women. Both signs share earthy qualities and a practical approach to life, fostering a strong and stable connection.

6. How do Capricorn women handle finances?

- Capricorn women are usually prudent with finances. They have the ability to accumulate wealth through practical investments and responsible financial management.

7. What careers are suitable for Capricorn women?

- Capricorn women thrive in careers that require responsibility, discipline, and strategic planning. They may excel in fields such as business, finance, law, or management.

8. How do Capricorn women handle challenges in life?

- Capricorn women face challenges with a determined and resilient attitude. They learn from their experiences, embrace personal growth, and navigate obstacles with a sense of responsibility.

9. Do Capricorn women believe in long-term commitments?

- Yes, Capricorn women value long-term commitments. They seek stability and security in relationships, often aiming for a lasting and meaningful connection.

10. How do Capricorn women balance work and personal life?

- Capricorn women are adept at balancing work and personal life. They prioritize their responsibilities and manage their time efficiently, ensuring they can succeed in both areas.

Frequently Asked Questions About Capricorn Men:

1. What are the typical personality traits of Capricorn men?

- Capricorn men are known for their traditional and serious nature. They possess a strong sense of independence, are skilled in self-control, and often make realistic plans.

2. How do Capricorn men behave in relationships?

- Capricorn men approach relationships with a sense of responsibility. They learn from their mistakes, rely on their experience, and are committed to making significant progress in their personal lives.

3. What is the ruling planet of Capricorn men and its influence?

- The ruling planet of Capricorn men is Saturn, representing restriction. While it makes them practical and responsible, it can also make them appear reserved. Forgiveness is essential for Capricorn men to lighten their lives.

4. Can you trust a Capricorn man?

- Capricorn men are generally trustworthy and reliable. They value commitment and stability in relationships, making them dependable partners.

5. What is the ideal match for a Capricorn man?

- Virgo is often considered an ideal match for Capricorn men. Both signs share earthy qualities and a practical approach to life, fostering a strong and stable connection.

6. How do Capricorn men handle finances?

- Capricorn men are usually prudent with finances. They have the ability to accumulate wealth through practical investments and responsible financial management.

7. What careers are suitable for Capricorn men?

- Capricorn men thrive in careers that require responsibility, discipline, and strategic planning. They may excel in fields such as business, finance, law, or management.

8. How do Capricorn men handle challenges in life?

- Capricorn men face challenges with a determined and resilient attitude. They learn from their experiences, embrace personal growth, and navigate obstacles with a sense of responsibility.

9. Do Capricorn men believe in long-term commitments?

- Yes, Capricorn men value long-term commitments. They seek stability and security in relationships, often aiming for a lasting and meaningful connection.

10. How do Capricorn men balance work and personal life?

- Capricorn men are adept at balancing work and personal life. They prioritize their responsibilities and manage their time efficiently, ensuring they can succeed in both areas.

Capricorn Turn-Ons:

Capricorn individuals, like everyone else, have specific characteristics and behaviors that can be considered turn-ons. Understanding what appeals to a Capricorn can enhance compatibility and strengthen relationships. Here are some key turn-ons for Capricorns:

1. Ambition and Drive:

- Capricorns are naturally ambitious and driven individuals. Seeing a partner who shares similar qualities and is focused on achieving goals can be a significant turn-on.

2. Discipline and Self-Control:

- Capricorns appreciate individuals who exhibit discipline and self-control. The ability to manage impulses and maintain composure is attractive to them.

3. Responsible and Reliable Behavior:

- Being responsible and reliable is a major turn-on for Capricorns. They value partners who fulfill their commitments and can be counted on in both personal and professional aspects.

4. Practicality in Daily Life:

- Capricorns are practical individuals who appreciate partners with a grounded approach to life. Practicality in decision-making and problem-solving can be a turn-on for them.

5. Financial Stability:

- Capricorns value financial stability and prudence. A partner who is financially responsible and shares similar values regarding money management can be appealing.

6. Sense of Humor:

- While Capricorns are known for their serious nature, they do appreciate a good sense of humor. A partner who can bring laughter and joy into their lives is likely to be a turn-on.

7. Demonstrating Long-Term Commitment:

- Capricorns are committed individuals and are attracted to partners who share a similar commitment to long-term relationships. Demonstrating loyalty and dedication can be highly appealing.

8. Intellectual Stimulation:

- Capricorns are drawn to individuals who can engage them intellectually. Stimulating conversations and sharing insightful thoughts can be a turn-on for these earthy individuals.

9. Thoughtful Gestures:

- Thoughtful gestures and acts of kindness resonate well with Capricorns. Small, considerate actions that show thoughtfulness can be particularly attractive.

10. Respect for Tradition:

- Capricorns often have a strong respect for tradition. A partner who appreciates and respects traditional values may find favor with a Capricorn.

11. Well-Groomed and Polished Appearance:

- Capricorns appreciate individuals who take care of their appearance. A well-groomed and polished look can be attractive to them.

12. **Supportive Nature:**

- Capricorns value support in their endeavors. A partner who is supportive of their goals and provides encouragement can be a turn-on.

Remember that individual preferences vary, and not every Capricorn will be attracted to the same qualities. Communication and understanding each other's preferences play a crucial role in building a strong and satisfying relationship.

Capricorn Turn-Offs:

Just like any other zodiac sign, Capricorns have certain traits and behaviors that can be considered turn-offs. While individual preferences vary, here are some common turn-offs for Capricorns:

1. **Lack of Ambition:**

- Capricorns are ambitious individuals, and they may be turned off by a lack of drive or ambition in a partner.

2. **Irresponsibility:**

- Irresponsible behavior, whether in personal or financial matters, can be a significant turn-off for Capricorns who value responsibility.

3. **Unreliability:**

- Capricorns appreciate reliability and commitment. Being consistently unreliable or breaking commitments can be off-putting to them.

4. **Impulsiveness:**

- Capricorns are known for their careful and calculated approach to life. Impulsive decision-making or actions may not align well with their preferences.

5. **Disregard for Tradition:**

- Capricorns often have a respect for tradition. Partners who disregard or dismiss traditional values may find it challenging to connect with a Capricorn.

6. **Lack of Self-Control:**

- Capricorns value self-control, and partners who struggle to manage their emotions or impulses may be seen as less attractive.

7. **Negative Attitude:**

- A consistently negative or pessimistic attitude can be a turn-off for Capricorns who prefer a more positive and pragmatic approach.

8. **Messiness and Disorganization:**

- Capricorns appreciate order and organization. A consistently messy or disorganized environment may not appeal to their sense of structure.

9. Lack of Long-Term Vision:

- Capricorns are forward-thinking and value long-term commitments. A partner who lacks a vision for the future may find it challenging to connect with them.

10. Unwillingness to Learn and Grow:

- Capricorns are constantly learning and growing. A partner who is resistant to personal development or growth may not align well with their values.

11. Poor Time Management:

- Capricorns are generally good at managing their time efficiently. Constant lateness or poor time management skills may be a turn-off.

12. Disrespectful Behavior:

- Disrespectful behavior towards them or others is likely to be a significant turn-off for Capricorns, who value mutual respect in relationships.

It's important to note that individual preferences vary, and effective communication is key in understanding each other's needs and boundaries within a relationship.

Preferred Gifts for Capricorn:

When selecting gifts for Capricorns, consider their practical and goal-oriented nature. Here are some suggestions for both him and her:

For Him:

1. **Quality Leather Accessories:**

- Capricorns often appreciate well-crafted items. Consider a high-quality leather wallet, belt, or a set of leather accessories.

2. **Classic Watch:**

- A classic and timeless watch can be a thoughtful gift for a Capricorn man. Opt for a design that aligns with his style.

3. **Professional Briefcase or Laptop Bag:**

- A stylish and functional briefcase or laptop bag can be a practical gift for the Capricorn man who is often on the go.

4. **Gourmet Food Basket:**

- Capricorns enjoy indulging in quality food. Put together a gourmet food basket with his favorite treats or fine dining items.

5. Book by a Respected Author:

- If he enjoys reading, consider a book by a respected author or a piece of literature related to his interests.

6. Investment in a Hobby:

- Identify his hobbies and consider a gift that supports or enhances one of his interests, such as quality golf accessories or equipment for a hobby he enjoys.

For Her:

1. Classic Jewelry:

- Capricorn women often appreciate timeless and classic jewelry pieces. Consider a pair of elegant earrings or a simple, sophisticated necklace.

2. Luxurious Skincare Set:

- Treat her to a luxurious skincare set or beauty products. Capricorns appreciate self-care, and quality skincare items can be a thoughtful gift.

3. Practical Handbag:

- A practical yet stylish handbag that suits her daily needs can make for a great gift. Opt for a design that aligns with her fashion preferences.

4. Personalized Planner or Journal:

- Capricorns are known for their organizational skills. A personalized planner or journal can be a useful and thoughtful gift.

5. Fine Perfume or Fragrance Set:

- Choose a high-quality perfume or fragrance set from a reputable brand. Capricorns often appreciate refined scents.

6. Cookware or Kitchen Gadgets:

- If she enjoys cooking or spending time in the kitchen, consider gifting high-quality cookware or innovative kitchen gadgets.

Remember to consider the individual tastes and interests of the Capricorn you're buying for, as personal preferences can vary widely. Tailoring the gift to their specific likes and needs will make it even more meaningful.

zodiacs adversaries to capricorn

The zodiac signs that are considered adversaries or have challenging relationships with Capricorn are primarily Aries, Gemini, and Libra. Let's explore the dynamics between Capricorn and these signs:

1. Aries (March 21 - April 19):

- Aries and Capricorn are both strong-willed and have leadership qualities, but their approaches can clash. Aries is impulsive and prefers to take risks, while Capricorn is more cautious and strategic. Aries may find Capricorn too conservative, and Capricorn may see Aries as too reckless.

2. Gemini (May 21 - June 20):

- Gemini's adaptable and changeable nature may be at odds with Capricorn's desire for stability and order. Capricorns tend to be practical and focused on long-term goals, while Geminis can be more scattered and unpredictable. Communication styles may also differ, leading to misunderstandings.

3. Libra (September 23 - October 22):

- Capricorn and Libra may struggle to find common ground. Capricorn is pragmatic and values hard work, while Libra seeks balance and harmony. Libra's indecisiveness may frustrate Capricorn, who prefers clear plans and goals. The two may have different priorities in relationships and social interactions.

It's essential to remember that individual compatibility depends on the entire birth chart, and many factors influence relationships. While these signs may present challenges, successful relationships can still be formed with open communication, understanding, and mutual respect.

Who Gets on Best with of

Certainly! Let's explore which zodiac signs tend to get along best with Capricorn:

1. Taurus (April 20 - May 20):

- Taurus and Capricorn share the Earth element, which makes them compatible. Both signs appreciate stability, security, and practicality. They understand each other's work ethic and commitment to long-term goals, fostering a strong and grounded connection.

2. Virgo (August 23 - September 22):

- Virgo and Capricorn are both ruled by Mercury, emphasizing intellect and practicality. They share a similar approach to life, focusing on details, organization, and efficiency. This compatibility creates a harmonious and supportive partnership.

3. Scorpio (October 23 - November 21):

- While Scorpio and Capricorn have different elemental influences (Water for

Scorpio and Earth for Capricorn), they share a deep and intense nature. Both signs value loyalty and commitment, creating a strong bond. Their shared determination helps them overcome challenges together.

4. **Pisces (February 19 - March 20):**

- Pisces and Capricorn may seem like an unlikely pair, but their differences can complement each other. Pisces brings creativity, intuition, and emotional depth, balancing Capricorn's practicality. When they communicate effectively, they can create a well-rounded and supportive partnership.

5. **Cancer (June 21 - July 22):**

- Cancer and Capricorn form a complementary axis in the zodiac, representing home and career. Cancer's nurturing and emotional nature blends well with Capricorn's ambition and determination. Together, they create a harmonious balance between work and emotional well-being.

It's important to note that individual birth charts play a significant role in relationship dynamics. While certain zodiac signs may generally get along better with Capricorn, successful relationships depend on communication, mutual understanding, and respect for each other's differences.

Attractive Traits

Capricorns are known for possessing a unique set of traits that many find attractive. Here are some of the qualities that make Capricorns appealing:

1. **Ambition:**

- Capricorns are highly ambitious and goal-oriented. Their drive to succeed and achieve their objectives can be inspiring and attractive to others.

2. **Discipline:**

- Capricorns are disciplined and hardworking individuals. They have a strong sense of responsibility and are committed to putting in the effort required to reach their goals.

3. **Reliability:**

- People are drawn to Capricorns because of their reliability. They are dependable and can be counted on to fulfill their commitments and responsibilities.

4. **Practicality:**

- Capricorns approach life with a practical mindset. Their ability to assess situations realistically and make sensible decisions is appreciated by those around them.

5. **Intelligence:**

- Capricorns are often intelligent and have a keen analytical mind. Their ability to think critically and solve problems adds to their attractiveness.

6. **Organizational Skills:**

- Capricorns are known for their organizational skills. They can create order out of chaos, which can be particularly appealing in both personal and professional settings.

7. **Sense of Humor:**

- Despite their serious demeanor, many Capricorns have a dry and witty sense of humor. This unexpected trait can make them charming and enjoyable to be around.

8. **Loyalty:**

- Capricorns value loyalty in their relationships and friendships. Their commitment to those they care about is a trait that others find endearing.

9. Independence:

- Capricorns are independent individuals who are comfortable standing on their own. This self-sufficiency can be attractive to those who appreciate autonomy.

10. Resilience:

- Capricorns are resilient in the face of challenges. Their ability to persevere and bounce back from setbacks is a strength that others find admirable.

11. Sophistication:

- Capricorns often have a sense of sophistication and class. Their refined tastes and manners contribute to an attractive and polished demeanor.

While these traits are associated with Capricorns, it's essential to remember that individuals are unique, and not every Capricorn will exhibit the same characteristics to the same degree. People are attracted to a variety of qualities, and compatibility often depends on the specific dynamics of individual relationships.

Negative traits

Like all zodiac signs, Capricorns have both positive and negative traits. While the positive traits contribute to their attractiveness, it's essential to be aware of potential challenges associated with the negative aspects. Here are some negative traits that Capricorns may exhibit:

1. **Stubbornness:**

- Capricorns can be stubborn and resistant to change. Their commitment to stability and tradition may make it challenging for them to adapt to new ideas or perspectives.

2. **Pessimism:**

- In certain situations, Capricorns may lean towards pessimism. Their realistic outlook can sometimes border on negativity, especially when faced with uncertainties.

3. **Overly Serious:**

- Capricorns are known for their serious and reserved nature. While this can be an asset in professional settings, it may lead to a lack of spontaneity and playfulness in personal relationships.

4. **Workaholic Tendencies:**

- Due to their strong work ethic, Capricorns may be prone to workaholic tendencies. This can lead to neglect of personal relationships and a focus solely on career goals.

5. **Rigidity:**

- Capricorns value structure and routine, but this can sometimes translate into rigidity. They may struggle to adapt when situations require flexibility.

6. **Materialistic:**

- Capricorns are often focused on achieving financial stability and success. In some cases, this can lead to materialistic tendencies, where they place too much emphasis on material possessions.

7. **Reserved Emotions:**

- Capricorns may struggle to express their emotions openly. Their reserved nature can make it challenging for them to communicate their feelings, leading to misunderstandings in relationships.

8. Cautious to a Fault:

- While being cautious is generally an asset, Capricorns may be overly cautious, which can hinder them from taking necessary risks or seizing opportunities.

9. Social Distance:

- Capricorns may keep a certain distance in social situations. Their reserved demeanor can make it difficult for others to get to know them on a deeper, more personal level.

10. Demanding Standards:

- Capricorns often have high standards, both for themselves and others. This can lead to frustration and disappointment if those standards are not met.

It's important to remember that these traits can vary among individuals, and not all Capricorns will display the same negative characteristics. Self-awareness and open communication can help Capricorns navigate these traits and foster healthier relationships.

Tailored Self-Care Practices Based on Your Zodiac Sign

Certainly! Here are tailored self-care practices based on the characteristics of Capricorn:

Capricorn (December 22 - January 19): Capricorns are known for their disciplined and hardworking nature. They often prioritize their responsibilities and may neglect self-care. Here are tailored self-care practices for Capricorns:

1. **Schedule "Me Time":**

- Capricorns are diligent schedulers. Set aside dedicated time for self-care activities in your calendar. Treat this time with the same importance as your work or other responsibilities.

2. **Set Achievable Goals:**

- While ambitious goals drive Capricorns, ensure your self-care goals are achievable. Break them down into smaller tasks, making it easier to accomplish and reducing unnecessary stress.

3. **Nature Walks:**

- Capricorns find solace in nature. Take a break from your routine and go for a nature walk. Whether it's a hike in the mountains or a stroll in a local park, reconnecting with nature can be rejuvenating.

4. **Mindfulness Practices:**

- Incorporate mindfulness practices into your daily routine. Whether it's meditation, deep breathing exercises, or yoga, these practices can help you stay grounded and reduce stress.

5. **Treat Yourself:**

- Capricorns often deserve a reward for their hard work. Treat yourself to something special, whether it's a favorite meal, a spa day, or indulging in a hobby you love.

6. **Unplug Regularly:**

- Capricorns can be workaholics. Set boundaries for yourself by unplugging from work-related activities regularly. This could mean turning off emails and work notifications during specific hours.

7. **Creative Outlets:**

- Explore creative outlets that allow you to express yourself. Whether it's writing, painting, or playing a musical instrument, engaging in creative activities can be a fulfilling form of self-care.

8. **Socialize Mindfully:**

- While Capricorns may not be the most social, it's essential to maintain meaningful connections. Choose quality over quantity in your social interactions, spending time with those who truly uplift and support you.

9. **Reflect and Plan:**

- Capricorns enjoy planning for the future. Take time to reflect on your achievements and set new goals. This process can provide a sense of direction and purpose.

10. **Pamper Your Body:**

- Capricorns may carry tension in their bodies due to stress. Treat yourself to massages, hot baths, or any form of physical pampering to release tension and promote relaxation.

Remember, self-care is crucial for maintaining overall well-being. By incorporating these practices into your routine, you can enhance your mental, emotional, and physical health as a Capricorn.

Ideal Dating Places For Your Partner's Zodiac Sign

Expressing your love and appreciation for your partner is essential, especially in a fast-paced world where success and achievements often take center stage. Whether you've just met, have been dating for a while, or are in a long-term relationship or marriage, your partner will always cherish an expression of your genuine emotions. Having a partner by your side reminds you of your humanity, and it's equally important to make them feel valued in your life.

One of the best ways to show your partner that they hold a special place in your heart is by taking them out on a date. There are 12 zodiac signs, each with unique personality traits that influence their romantic preferences. Some share common traits, while others are entirely distinct from one another.

In this article, we will explore ideal dating places for each zodiac sign. If you're uncertain about your Ascendant zodiac sign, Indastro can help you determine it, enabling you to discover the perfect dating spots that align with your personality and make a great first impression, especially if it's your first date!

Aries, Scorpio, Sagittarius, and Pisces

These zodiac signs (ascendants) are highly romantic and enjoy open spaces. They have a natural inclination toward engaging in activities, making a picnic in a beautiful park or dining at open terrace restaurants surrounded by lush greenery an ideal date for them.

As adrenaline junkies, they are drawn to sports that align with their partner's interests, such as trekking and water rafting. Engaging in such activities keeps them on the edge of their seats and fills them with elation. A romantic beach stroll is a top choice for these signs, offering both romance and relaxation.

They also have a penchant for nightlife, making a night club or a late-night movie a frequent choice for their dates.

Taurus, Gemini, Virgo, and Libra

For these ascendants, emotional connection holds more significance than the venue itself. They value the genuine emotions, loyalty, and dedication of their partner over extravagant settings. An ideal date for them involves being in the company of someone with whom they can freely and openly communicate, without the need for extensive planning.

These individuals are highly adaptable, and any location chosen by their partner is perfect for them. If asked to make a choice, they often prefer quiet and peaceful places for their dates, where they can comfortably relax with their lover and engage in uninterrupted conversations. They have an affinity for various types of flowers, appreciating their different fragrances and colors.

While they may harbor deep feelings for someone, expressing those emotions can be a challenge. It takes time for them to muster the courage to share their love openly.

Cancer, Leo, Capricorn, and Aquarius

Long drives and trips epitomize the ideal dates for these ascendants. They are a highly dynamic bunch and dislike staying in one place, even during a date. They are deeply enamored with motion, making a long drive or a short trip to a distant location their idea of a great date. These individuals are enthusiastic about nightlife and enjoy vibrant and loud music, so don't be surprised if they invite you to a nightclub or a concert.

These ideal dating places cater to the unique personality traits of each zodiac sign, ensuring a memorable and enjoyable experience for both you and your partner. Whether you're exploring open spaces, seeking emotional connection, or embarking on exciting adventures, understanding your partner's zodiac sign can enhance your dating experiences and strengthen your bond.

"Unveiling the Romantic Essence of Every Zodiac Sign" how romantic they are

Aries - The Adventurous Romantic: Aries, represented by the fearless Ram, is known for their determination, strength, and bold energy. Their approach to love mirrors their impulsive nature as they fearlessly dive into challenging situations. In relationships, Aries individuals remain true to themselves and do not accommodate easily, making them moderate romantics who crave excitement.

Taurus - The Stable Romantic: Symbolized by the steadfast Bull, Taurus is an Earth sign seeking stability and comfort in love. Their loyalty and commitment attract partners, creating enduring romances. Taurus natives thrive in serene settings, surrounded by music, delightful food, and comforting scents, making them ideal for long-lasting love.

Gemini - The Cynical Romantic: Gemini, represented by the celestial twins, is an airy sign in perpetual pursuit of new experiences. While they bring a sense of variety and curiosity to relationships, their dual personalities can make them indecisive and emotionally vulnerable at times. To unlock their full romantic potential, Geminis need compatible partners.

Cancer - The Incredibly Romantic: As a water sign symbolized by the Crab, Cancer deftly transitions between emotional and materialistic aspects. Nurturers at heart, Cancer individuals understand their partners' desires and provide unwavering support, patience, and unconditional love. They embody the essence of a true romantic.

Leo - The Authentic Romantic: Leo, a fiery sign represented by the Lion, exudes vivacity, passion, and regal charisma. Their chivalry and passion attract admirers, but Leo's need for independence may pose challenges for some. They celebrate themselves and the idea of being in love, making them charismatic romantics.

Virgo - The Perfectionist in Romance: Virgo, symbolized by the Virgin, embodies purity and practicality. Their systematic approach to life extends to love, making them attentive listeners and loyal partners. They give their all in love and offer a refreshingly detailed perspective, making them perfect romantics.

Libra - The Demanding Romantic: Represented by the scales, Libra seeks balance in life. Their sociable nature and desire for reciprocity in love make them excellent romantics. They care for everyone and their partnerships, demanding symmetry in their relationships.

Scorpio - The Passionately Romantic: Scorpio, symbolized by the Scorpion, is a complex sign with fiery and watery traits. They struggle with trust issues but harbor intense emotions. Scorpios offer unparalleled passion and sensuality in love, creating deep connections with their partners.

Sagittarius - The Classic Unoriginal Romantic: Sagittarius, represented by the Archer, is known for its energy and pursuit of knowledge. They protect their partners and prioritize safety. While they may struggle to express themselves, they excel at understanding their partner's needs, adding a classic touch to romance.

Capricorn - The Realistic and Sincere Romantic: The last earthy sign, Capricorn, symbolized by the Goat, values tradition and seeks perfection in love. They are honest, responsible, and loyal partners, creating powerful romantic connections. They aim for confidence and power in their relationships.

Aquarius - The Carefree Romantic: Despite its name, Aquarius, an airy sign, focuses on humanitarianism and personal growth. Their carefree approach to romance values honesty and independence. They may not be traditional romantics but appreciate honesty in relationships.

Pisces - The Hopeless Romantic: The last sign of the zodiac, Pisces, a water sign with two fish, embodies compassion and love. They believe in fairy-tale romance, openly sharing their feelings with partners. Pisces individuals are dedicated and embrace the concept of "happily ever after."

Zodiac Sign	Type of Attraction	Attraction Skills
Aries	Adventurous romantic	4
Taurus	Stable romantic	5
Gemini	Cynical romantic	3
Cancer	Incredibly Romantic	5
Leo	Authentic romantic	4
Virgo	Perfectionist in romance	4
Libra	Demanding Romantic	4

Scorpio | *Passionately Romantic* | *3*

Sagittarius | *Classic Unoriginal Romantic* | *4*

Capricorn | *Realistic and Sincere Romantic* | *4*

Aquarius | *Carefree Romantic* | *3*

Pisces | *Hopeless Romantic* | *5*

What is the zodiac?

The zodiac is an astronomical coordinate system that divides the ecliptic, the apparent path of the Sun across the celestial sphere, into twelve equal zones known as zodiac signs. These signs are named after constellations that lie along the ecliptic. The zodiac is widely used in astrology, a belief system that suggests a relationship between the positions of celestial bodies and events on Earth, including human life and personality traits.

As mentioned in your provided information, there are two primary astrological zodiacs: the Tropical Western zodiac and the Sidereal Vedic zodiac.

Tropical Western Zodiac:

Based on the position of the Sun, the Tropical Western zodiac divides the ecliptic into twelve signs of equal 30-degree segments. It is primarily associated with Western astrology, where the positions of planets are fixed in relation to the Sun. The Western zodiac is often used for horoscopes and personality analysis.

Sidereal Vedic Zodiac:

The Sidereal Vedic zodiac is based on the actual observed positions of the stars and planets in the sky. It divides the ecliptic into twelve unequal segments, with each sign corresponding to the constellation it is named after. This system is primarily associated with Vedic or Indian astrology and is known for its emphasis on the Moon's influence on emotions.

The primary difference lies in the reference point for the division of the zodiac. The Western system is Sun-centered (tropical), while the Vedic system is star-centered (sidereal) and places importance on lunar positions.

Astrology, using either zodiac system, is often perceived as a tool to gain insights into individuals' personalities, behaviors, and potential life events. It involves creating natal charts based on the positions of celestial bodies at the time of a person's birth. Astrologers interpret these charts to provide insights into various aspects of a person's life, including relationships, career, and personal growth.

Why is astrology so provocative?

Astrology is often considered provocative for several reasons, rooted in a combination of cultural, religious, and personal perspectives. Here are some reasons why astrology might be perceived as provocative:

Belief Systems and Skepticism:

Astrology involves the belief that celestial bodies' positions at the time of a person's birth can influence their personality, behavior, and life events. Skeptics often challenge the scientific validity of astrology, leading to debates between believers and non-believers.

Religious Differences:

Astrology operates outside the realm of many religious doctrines, and some religious beliefs may view it as incompatible or contradictory. For individuals with strong religious convictions, the practice of astrology can be seen as provocative or even conflicting.

Determinism vs. Free Will:

The idea that astrological charts can predict future events raises questions about determinism versus free will. Some people find the notion of predetermined life events uncomfortable, challenging the concept of personal agency and decision-making.

Categorization and Generalization:

Astrology often involves categorizing individuals into specific personality types based on their zodiac signs. Critics argue that this categorization can lead to oversimplification and generalization, overlooking the complexity of individual personalities.

Cultural Variances:

Different cultures have varying perspectives on astrology. While some cultures embrace and incorporate astrological practices into daily life, others may reject them entirely. This cultural diversity contributes to differing opinions on the validity and acceptability of astrology.

Despite these points of contention, there are individuals who find value and fascination in astrology. Some appreciate it as a tool for self-reflection, personal growth, or even as a lens through which to interpret world events. Astrology, particularly Vedic astrology, is seen by some as a means of gaining insights into oneself and the world, providing a unique perspective on interconnectedness and cosmic influences.

As with many belief systems, the acceptance or rejection of astrology often depends on personal experiences, cultural backgrounds, and individual worldviews. Open-mindedness, as mentioned, allows for the exploration of diverse perspectives and the potential for eye-opening realizations.

Astrology's Role in Predicting Daily Life Events

Believe it or not, astrology plays a significant role in deciphering our daily lives. By delving into our history and considering the alignment of planets at specific times, astrologers can draw connections between past events and current planetary positions. This historical perspective is crucial for understanding future opportunities and potential challenges.

Astrology, with its roots dating back to the 3rd millennium BC, has stood the test of time. This ancient practice provides a unique lens through which individuals can gain insights into the cyclical nature of celestial movements and their potential impact on daily life events.

Navigating Zodiac Mismatch: Western vs. Vedic Astrology

Ever felt like your zodiac sign doesn't quite capture your essence? Well, you might be delving into the realm of Western astrology, commonly consulted for insights on ideal partners or job prospects. The Western zodiac comprises Aries, Taurus,

Gemini, Cancer, Leo, Virgo, Libra, Scorpio, Sagittarius, Capricorn, Aquarius, and Pisces.

As you explore this article, you might be thinking, "Can the astrological zodiac really predict the future if it can't nail my personality traits?" According to experts like White, the discrepancy is entirely normal. In Western astrology, your sign on August 1 might label you a Leo, yet you might not resonate with that fiery energy. Enter Vedic astrology, which operates on a different calendar, placing you as a Cancer, a more sensitive designation due to a four-week variance.

The key might lie in aligning with one system more than the other. White suggests checking both Western and Vedic astrological interpretations to gain a comprehensive understanding of your celestial profile. It's a journey of self-discovery that acknowledges the diversity within astrological practices.

Why do the 12 zodiac signs begin with Aries and not Capricorn?

Aries Leading the Zodiac: Exploring the Cosmic Decision

Ever wondered why the 12 zodiac signs kick off with Aries and not Capricorn, especially when Capricorn aligns with the new year? It might seem a tad perplexing, given the zodiac's alignment with dates.

However, the zodiac is not merely a calendar but a cosmic narrative of the soul and its inner workings. Hence, it makes sense to have Aries, a sign synonymous with boldness and courage, take the lead. According to White, "Aries has always been known as bold and courageous—so it is first in the zodiac! Fearless for sure!"

So, while earthly calendars mark the beginning of the year with Capricorn, the celestial narrative of the zodiac embarks on its journey with the spirited and adventurous Aries. It's a cosmic decision that aligns with the essence of each sign and their distinctive attributes. Now, let's dive into the intriguing dates and traits that define each zodiac sign for a closer

Dear readers, as we wrap up our exploration of 'Exploring Capricorn: A Comprehensive Guide,' I hope this journey through the celestial landscapes of the Goat sign has been as enlightening for you as it has been for me.

Together, we've uncovered the mysteries behind Capricorn's origins, delved into the intricacies of its personality traits, and navigated the cosmic dance between this determined Earth sign and its celestial counterparts. From career paths to love dynamics, we've touched on every aspect of Capricorn's multifaceted existence.

As we bid adieu, remember that the stars above are not just distant dots; they are a reflection of the energies within us. Capricorns, with their resilience and unwavering determination, are a testament to the cosmic forces that shape our lives.

May this guide serve as a compass, helping you navigate the challenges and bask in the joys that 2024 and beyond have in store. Like a steadfast Goat climbing the mountain of dreams, may you scale new heights, overcome obstacles, and find fulfillment in every endeavor.

Thank you for joining me on this cosmic journey. Until we meet again under the starry skies, keep reaching for the stars and embracing the wisdom that the universe graciously bestows upon us.

Wishing you a celestial farewell,

Daniel Sanjurjo"

Contact the Astrologer

If you find yourself intrigued and eager to explore the depths of astrology further, whether for personal consultations or additional inquiries, our team is here to assist you.

Please don't hesitate to get in touch with us at:

Phone: +1 829-205-5456

WhatsApp

Email: danielsanjurjo47@gmail.com

Your feedback, questions, and insights are always encouraged, and we are excited to aid you in uncovering the distinct characteristics of each zodiac sign.

As you continue your celestial voyage through the realm of astrology, we wish you a future illuminated with clarity, self-discovery, and the enduring wisdom of the stars. The Scorpio zodiac sign has shared its unique insights with us, and we hope you carry that wisdom with you on your journey.

Once again, thank you for being a part of this incredible odyssey. We appreciate your readership, your inquisitiveness, and your shared enthusiasm for the zodiac.

With heartfelt thanks,

Daniel Sanjurjo

Did you love Cancer Zodiac Sign 2024? Then you should read The Dreams Interpretation Book[1] by Daniel Sanjurjo!

☐ Unlock the Secrets of Dreams with "Dreamscape Chronicles: A Journey into the World of Dreams"

☐ Are you ready to embark on a profound dream interpretation journey that will unveil the hidden meanings of your dreams, offering insights into your inner self, personal growth, and self-discovery? "Dreamscape Chronicles" is your definitive guide to navigating the enigmatic landscapes of the subconscious mind.

☐ Explore the Depths of Dream Analysis: Delve into the intricate world of dream interpretation, where the symbols and stories of the night come alive. From common dreams to the mysteries of the mind, this book unravels the symbolism and significance of your dreamscapes.

☐ Illuminate Your Path: Discover how dreams can inspire your creativity, provide therapeutic insights, and awaken your inner desires. This book serves as

your compass, guiding you through the rich tapestry of dreams and helping you harness their potential.

☐ Key Topics Explored: Uncover the significance of dream symbolism, the role of common dream themes, and the influence of pioneers like Sigmund

Freud in understanding the profound landscapes of the dreamer's mind.

Are you ready to embark on a journey through the dreamer's world? "Dreamscape Chronicles" is your passport to the boundless landscapes of your own mind. Explore, interpret, and awaken to the possibilities hidden within your dreams.

Unlock the mysteries of your dreams and start your journey of self-discovery today!

Also by Daniel Sanjurjo

Zodiac

Pisces 2024: Un Viaje Celestial

Zodiac world

Aries Revealed 2024

Taurus 2024 Leo 2024

Gemini 2024

Cancer Zodiac Sign 2024

Virgo 2024

Scorpio 2024

Sagittarius 2024 Horoscope

Capricorn Unveiled: A Cosmic Guide to 2024

Aquarius Horoscope 2024

Standalone

The Dreams Interpretation Book

About the Author

Daniel Sanjurjo is a passionate author who delves into the realms of astrology and self-help. With a gift for exploring the celestial and the human psyche, Daniel's books are celestial journeys of self-discovery and personal growth. Join the cosmic odyssey with this insightful writer.

Printed in Great Britain
by Amazon